About the Book

By the time you finish this book, you'll understand everything basic that's worth knowing about money—how to make it grow and how easily you can lose it. Here, entertainingly and with clarity, author Tom Morgan offers information that everyone should possess but many do not.

- Three people save $2,000 per year for 30 years. At the end of that time one has $60,000, one $120,000, one $245,000. What happened?
- Three people buy houses costing $25,000. One actually pays $25,000, one pays $42,000, one pays $50,000. Why?
- One man's grocery store goes broke and he closes up. Next day he goes on a spending spree around the world. How?

Here, with realistic dramatization of what can happen to anyone from school days on, you discover how basically simple are such things as stocks, bonds, and mortgages. It's vital knowledge that everyone should have, whether a high school student or an astrophysicist. In fact, next time you meet an astrophysicist, ask him to explain a second mortgage. Probably he won't be able to, but the simple answer is in these pages.

MONEY, MONEY, MONEY

HOW TO GET AND KEEP IT

TOM MORGAN

Illustrations by Joe Ciardiello

G. P. PUTNAM'S SONS, NEW YORK

Copyright © 1978 by Tom Morgan
All rights reserved. Published
simultaneously in Canada by
Longman Canada Limited, Toronto.
Printed in the United States of America
12 up

Library of Congress Cataloging in Publication Data
Morgan, Tom.
  Money, money, money.
  Includes index.
  1. Finance, Personal.   I. Title.
HG179.M65   1978   332'.024   78-1769
ISBN 0-399-20641-8

To my dad

Acknowledgments

My thanks to Barbara Elkema for typing and helping; to Claudia, Ann, and Nicole Elkema for reading; to Nan Kristensen for typing; to Jean for encouraging; to my neighbor Fred Lucchese, who plowed the snow from my driveway and thereby left me free to write this book; to Pamela, Benjamin, and Kathleen, who kept quiet while I wrote it.

CONTENTS

1. Money, Money, Money — 13
2. You Can't Eat It — 16
3. Banks Are Interest . . . ing — 19
4. Check into Checks — 32
5. It's Here, There, Everywhere — 37
6. Two's Company — 50
7. Gambling — 68
8. A Loan to Mickey Mouse — 75
9. Lend Me Your Ear — 81
10. A Word About Profits — 88
11. Money to Burn—or at Least Invest — 92
12. Inflation — 101
13. Bankruptcy — 106
14. What Now? — 111
    Index — 115

MONEY, MONEY, MONEY

1

MONEY, MONEY, MONEY

Let's look at three people who have money. They are similar to people you know, like relatives and friends. They are like the President of the United States and your favorite sports star.

Mr. Johnson saved $2,000 every year for 30 years. His neighbor, Mrs. Emery, did exactly the same. Her sister, Amy Brown, also saved $2,000 every year for 30 years.

For 30 years none of these people spent any of his or her savings. Each one set the money aside for the time when he or she could retire. So each one set aside a total of $60,000 over 30 years.

Last month each retired. Mr. Johnson had $60,000 for his retirement. But Mrs. Emery had $120,000 for hers. Meanwhile, Amy Brown had $245,000! How could this be? Did Mrs. Emery perform magic with her money? Was Amy Brown an even greater magician?

These people have other money differences. Mr. Johnson liked a house he saw. It was selling for $25,000. Mrs. Emery wanted to buy an apartment. Its price was $25,000, too. Amy Brown was attracted to a lovely condominium. She asked the owner if it was for sale. It was, for $25,000.

These people bought the residences they liked. The price tag on each residence was $25,000. Mr. Johnson paid exactly $25,000. Mrs. Emery paid $42,000. And Amy Brown parted with $50,000 for her condominium. What happened? Were Mrs. Emery and Amy Brown bilked?

These three people did some interesting things over the years with other money they earned. For instance, Mr. Johnson loaned money to a country: that's right, a nation. Mrs. Emery loaned some of her money to Disneyland. Amy Brown bought a part of CBS television, and CBS paid some money to her every year simply because she owned that part.

Mr. Johnson owned a grocery store for a while. The store did not make much money for him. Finally one year it did so poorly Mr. Johnson decided to close its doors forever. The store owed money to the companies that delivered bread and meat and fruit. When the store closed down, they demanded that Mr. Johnson pay the money. He told them he was sorry but the store was broke. It could not pay them. It could not pay the telephone company or the electric company the money it owed them either.

Some of Mr. Johnson's neighbors were upset. "Poor Mr. Johnson is broke," they sighed. "He's so poor he won't be able to buy clothes or food." They thought they might take up a collection for him.

However, the day after he closed the store Mr. Johnson bought a new car and new clothes. Then he took Mrs. Johnson on a vacation trip to Europe. He was completely honest. He didn't steal any money. He did not lie to the companies to which his store owed money either. Still, he went on a spending spree. How did he do it? Was he broke or wasn't he?

Meanwhile, Mrs. Emery loaned some money to a company one morning. It loaned some money back to her that afternoon. The company kept her money for five years. Mrs. Emery kept the company's money for three years. The company paid extra money back to Mrs. Emery. And she paid extra money to the company. They were both happy with the arrangement. What was going on?

You'll be able to answer all these questions by the time you finish this book.

2

YOU CAN'T EAT IT

Suppose you save all the money your parents give you and stash away all the cash you earn working odd jobs. You save up as much as $200, stuff the money in the toe of a shoe, and hide it under your bed, planning not to touch it for an entire year.

Next morning your best friend Sam asks if you'll lend him $200. Wouldn't you know it?

"You're crazy, Sam! Two hundred dollars? Where would I get money like that?"

"C'mon, I know you've been saving your money for a long time," Sam says. "You've got two hundred bucks. And I need the money for a very important project. I'll pay it back in exactly one year. You have my word. In fact, I'll sign a note that promises I'll return the money."

"Two hundred dollars is a lot of money, Sam," you remind him.

"Sure it is. But I'm your best friend, aren't I? Your very best friend. I'd lend you a thousand dollars if you needed it and I had it. I'd give you the shirt off my back. We're best friends, remember?"

"Let me think about it and tell you tomorrow."

At home you fish the bills out of the shoe, lay them on your bed, and think about Sam's request. What is he going to do with the money? What if he's run over by a truck? What happens to your money then? His note will be worthless because he'll be dead.

By morning you think you have a solution and decide to lend Sam the money. But because you will have worries and headaches about the money while he has it, you'll make him pay you for your troubles. Because you will be a bit envious, you'll have him cross your palm with silver to relieve your envy. You will not be able to use your money for a year, and so you'll make Sam pay you for this inconvenience.

You go to him and explain:

"I may want to use the money this year, but I won't be able to because you'll have it. And I might be envious of what you're doing with my money. I mean you might do something with it that I'd like to do. Or you might lose my money and not be able to pay me back. And you might fall into a canyon at a summer camp out West. You're going to cause me all these worries. I mean, I'm taking a risk, Sam. So you've got to reward me for this."

"Sounds reasonable," Sam admits. "How much do I have to reward you?"

You think about it for a moment. "How about fifty dollars?"

"Hey, that's too much of a reward!" exclaims Sam. "I can borrow money from Mike for twenty-five dollars."

"Oh, I didn't know. Twenty-five dollars, huh? Okay, how about twenty dollars?"

"It's a deal. When I return your two hundred dollars, I'll give you an extra twenty dollars for letting me use it."

What you've just worked out with Sam is basically the same as most of the money transactions that occurred in the world today. They took place in banks and stock markets and various financial institutions. They had fancy names which you may not understand yet. Still, they were basically the same as your $200 loan to Sam.

Nearly every financial transaction has this in common with your deal with Sam: Someone wants to use someone else's money. That someone else wants to be paid for his worries. He wants to be paid for the risk he takes when he lets another someone use his money. The more risk there is, the more he wants to be paid for the gamble.

Money is like seed. You can lend pea seeds to Sam. He can use them to grow plants. The plants will produce more pea seeds than he planted. (When you leave the peas in the pod and on the plant for a long time they harden into seed.) Sam can then return the same amount of seeds he borrowed and some extra.

Suppose you want to keep your seeds instead? You can plant them in the garden or in window boxes. Each seed will grow into a plant. Each plant will produce more seeds. In this way you will increase the number of seeds you own. Or you can give your seeds to a friend to grow, with one stipulation: He has to pay you with some peas out of every harvest. Beyond that he can do what he wants with the seeds. Or you can keep your pea seeds stuffed in the toe of your shoe.

Your money is like seed, except you can't eat it.

3

BANKS ARE INTEREST...ING

Suppose that, instead of keeping your $200 in your shoe, you put it in a bank.

If your house burns while you're away, your shoe and your $200 go up in flames. At the bank the flames can't get at your money because it's in a fireproof vault. Or, if a thief breaks into your house, he may find and take your money. But the money is safe in the bank.

When your money is in a bank, you can still get it when you want it. It's not as easy to get as when it's in your shoe, for the bank is closed at night and on Sundays. Your shoe is open all the time. Still, you don't have to wait very long to retrieve your money from a bank.

There are other advantages to a bank. It keeps you from spending money too freely; if you carried all this money with you, you'd be more tempted to spend it than if it was in a bank. But the best thing about a bank is that it *pays* you for depositing your money there. These days the bank will pay you five cents for every dollar left there for a year.

The bank pays you this money for the same reason Sam was willing to pay $20 for your $200. It wants to *borrow* your money. If you lend the money, it will pay you for doing so. The money it pays you is called "interest." The $20 Sam is willing to pay you is the same—interest.

We talk about interest in percentages rather than dollars. Sam, then, will pay you 10% interest. (10% × $200 = $20) The bank today will pay you from 4% to 7%, maybe even 8%, interest. The exact percentage it pays depends on a few things we'll discuss later.

Let's say the bank pays you 5% interest every year on your $200. Where does it get the money to pay you the 5% interest? The answer is simple. It lends your $200 to others for more interest than for what you lend it to the bank.

For instance, it will lend Sam the $200 he wants and charge him 12% interest. It may lend your neighbor the money he needs for a new car. It charges him 12% (or maybe more) interest.

So the bank pays you 5% for the $200, or $10. It lends Sam the $200 and charges him 12%, or $24. The difference is 7%, or $14. The bank makes a 7% profit on your money this year. It makes a $14 profit.

That may not seem to you like a lot of profit. But if a bank will borrow $200 from 100,000 people, this will give it $20,000,000 to lend. If it lends it to hundreds or thousands of Sams at 12%, it makes a profit of 7%. Multiply 7% × $20,000,000 = $1,400,000. Not bad.

You can understand why it is important for a bank to lend all or most of its money all year long. Every year it has to pay 5% interest to you and other depositors, no matter what it does with your money. So it doesn't want to leave much of it lying around the vault, sleeping. It wants to make it earn its keep. It lends it out, makes it work, in order to earn interest.

Why do we need banks? Or do we need them at all?

To help answer that question, answer this: If Sam wants to borrow $5,000, will you lend it to him? Of course not. You don't have that much money. And if you did, you'd probably be afraid to lend that much money to one person.

If there were no banks and Sam needed $5,000, he'd have to ask dozens of people to lend him money. It would take a lot of his time and be quite complicated for him. He'd no doubt prefer to go to one place and borrow the entire $5,000. So do students who need $10,000 to go to college. So do people who want to borrow $50,000 to buy a home. So do companies that wish to borrow $500,000 to build a factory.

That is why banks exist. They put together $200 from you, $100 from your friend, $300 from your uncle, until they have huge amounts of money together. Then they lend it to people and companies and organizations and countries. They lend it in large and small amounts. They collect interest for what they lend. They pay smaller amounts of interest for what they borrow. The differences between the two interests is their profit. They use the profit to buy their buildings and vaults and to pay their employees. Whoever owns the bank gets some of what's left over after that.

There are different banks for different purposes.

Suppose there are lots of Sams who want to borrow money in

your school and there are lots of people who have saved their money. If it were legal, everyone might get together and create a Youth Bank. The bank could deposit savings and pay interest while lending money to other students. It would be a Youth Bank. There are a few of these around the country.

Now suppose several manufacturers want to create a bank which will amass money and lend it to manufacturers like themselves when they need it. They want a bank able to lend very large amounts of money, for companies naturally need large loans for big projects such as new factories. They may create an Industrial Bank.

Or suppose there are farmers who want a bank which will lend them money to build new barns. They want a Farmers' Bank because it might understand better why farmers need to borrow money. The Farmers' Bank will be required to lend most of its money to farmers.

Or suppose that blacks want a Black Bank. "Hey, many of us blacks are poor," they say. They need to borrow money, but most regular banks don't lend them much money. "Those banks prefer to lend to wealthier people, who are more likely to pay the money back. We want a bank which will loan most of its money to us. We want it to loan money to blacks who want to start businesses. We want a Black Bank."

Or suppose several countries want a bank to lend money to poor countries and new countries. They want a World Bank. The amounts it loans will be colossal—millions of dollars at a time—and the risks will be high.

All of these and many more special banks exist. There are black banks, farm banks, Indian banks, rancher banks, chemical banks. There is even a World Bank. But all operate in the same way. They borrow money from their depositors and pay them low interest. Then they turn around and lend the money and charge high interest for lending it.

The rate of interest is not the same from one year to the next. The bank may pay you 5% interest on your savings this year. Next year it might pay only 4½%. The bank may charge Sam 12% for his loan this year. Next year it might charge him only 11% for an identical loan. What's happening?

Remember when you had to lower your interest rate for Sam? That's what's happening. You first wanted $50 interest (25%) from Sam for the $200 you were going to loan. When Sam found someone who'd let him borrow the money for only $25 interest (12½%), you settled for $20 (10%). There was simply too much money around that Sam could borrow cheaply. In fact, if there had been twenty of your classmates there with $200 each, Sam could have played all of you against one another.

If the shoe had been on the other foot, Sam would not have been able to wheel and deal. But you could have. Suppose only you had $200 to lend. And twenty guys like Sam wanted to borrow it.

"How much interest?" Sam would have asked.

"Fifty dollars."

"What? That's twenty-five percent. You're nuts."

"I'm also rich, Sam. Nobody else has money to lend. Take it or leave it, Sam. Mike'll give me forty-three dollars interest. Sally will give me forty-seven dollars. Hey, Sam, who needs you?"

"Some pal you are. Okay, fifty dollars interest."

Here the interest rate went up because there was a shortage of available money. When there was a surplus of money, the interest went down. You might hear somebody call this "supply and demand." Here's another example of it.

Let's say your mother sells new cars. She has a big showroom and sells cars for about $6,000. Then workers at the Ford factory go on strike. An earthquake destroys the Chrysler and General Motors factories. And there's a bad fire at an American Motors factory.

After all these calamities, nobody makes any cars for two years. But people still want to buy new cars. Some of them have to have new cars to get to work. They get desperate and are willing to pay extra money to make sure they get one of the few cars still left in the showrooms.

Your mother, being no dummy, raises her prices to $12,000. Sure enough, people come in and pay that much for her cars.

When there's not enough money in banks for people to borrow, some get desperate. They're willing to pay extra interest for loans. When this happens, the bank raises the interest rate on money it loans out.

Finally the strike ends. Ruined factories are rebuilt and start to make lots of cars. The whole country is enthusiastic. So is your mother, who lowers her price for a car back to $6,000. She buys lots of new cars, hundreds of them. All the other car dealers do the same. They're enthusiastic, too. They, like your mother, overspend and buy too many cars. Soon all dealers have far more cars than they can sell.

Before long customers start telling dealers they can get better buys from other dealers. And not long after that starts, your mother and other dealers begin offering cars at greatly reduced prices.

The bank does this, too, with money. Sometimes it has too

much money and can't loan all of it out at once. *When too much money begins to sit around not working for the bank, signs appear in the windows: "NEW LOW, LOW INTEREST RATES ON LOANS!" When the bank lowers the interest rate on loans it encourages more people to come in and ask for a loan.*

The bank does the same with the interest it pays you for money you lend to it. When it has more money than it can lend, it pays you a low interest—say 3% On the other hand, when it needs more money, it pays you higher interest—maybe 6%. It wants to tempt you to pull your savings out of your shoe and hotfoot it down to the bank.

Let's go back to Sam and the $200 he wants to borrow from you. Remember, he's going to pay $20 interest to borrow the $200 for one year.

He comes back next day with a new scheme. He wants to borrow the $200 for a little longer than a year.

"Five years! Did I hear you right, Sam? Five years?!"

"Hey, this is a big project. This is my five-year plan."

"Wow! Five years, eh?" You think about it. "Sam, that's a long time for me to be without my money. You're going to have to pay me thirty dollars interest every year."

Sam shrugs. "Worth it. Worth it. When I know that I can use that two hundred dollars for five whole years, it's worth the extra interest. I mean, now I can plan my project on a long-term basis. I don't have to worry about borrowing a new bundle of money every year. Worth it."

The bank feels the same way. If you promise to leave money in the bank (that is, to lend it to the bank) for a year, the bank may give you 4½% interest. If you agree to leave it three years

—maybe 5½% interest. If you agree to leave it five years— maybe 6½% interest.

You deserve the extra interest. You're going without your money for a long time. The bank should pay you extra interest. "Worth it," says the bank. *Now it can lend your money to people like Sam on three- or five-year loans.*

Suppose Sam wants to borrow $1,000 from you at 10% interest. You recoil. "Two hundred dollars at ten percent interest was one thing, Sam. But a thousand dollars is a different matter. It's a bigger risk. It's a bigger inconvenience. I'm going to insist on fifteen percent interest."

"Okay," says Sam. He's so agreeable today. "I could get a thousand dollars together at ten percent. But I'd probably have to go to five different people and get two hundred from each one. That takes time, and lots of persuading. And that's five written promises—five deals I'd have to keep track of. This is easier. One deal, one amount, one person to persuade. It's worth the extra interest."

The bank feels the same. If you deposit $200, the bank may pay you 4½% interest. If you deposit $5,000, it may pay 5½%. If you offer to deposit $500,000, the president of the bank may invite you in for coffee and offer you 7½% interest.

Imagine how easy it is for the bank to handle your $500,000 in one lump. It records the deposit on a few pieces of paper and gives you a bankbook. Meanwhile, when 1,000 people deposit $500 each, the bank receives $500,000, too. But it issues 1,000 bankbooks. It pays people to process thousands of pieces of paper. All of this is expensive. No wonder the bank is happy to pay you a higher rate of interest for your $500,000 deposit.

Suppose your school has the Youth Bank discussed earlier.

You and 49 others deposit $200 in it. This makes $10,000. The bank pays you 5% interest.

In order to pay out the 5% interest, it lends most of the money to dozens of others at 12%. It lends all but $1,000. It keeps that much to pay people who might suddenly want to take their money out of the bank.

Sam, one of the borrowers, wants $200 for his soft ice cream business. Mike and Sally are also borrowers. Mike borrows $100 for a bike, while Sally borrows $30 for six months to buy ice skates.

If things go wrong and none of them can repay their loans, will these losses ruin the bank?

Of course not. The Youth Bank still has $8,670 loaned all over the school. It makes 12% interest on those loans, or $1,040 this year alone. So it can afford these losses.

Nonetheless, rumors sweep through the school. Students whisper warnings to each other. "The bank's not going to have enough money. The bank's going broke."

Next day 25 students show up at the Youth Bank. They all want to withdraw their $200. That comes to $5,000. But the bank only keeps $1,000 around for withdrawals. The rest of the money is loaned out.

"We don't have enough money here for all of you," the bank manager tells the depositors.

They panic and spread the bad news through the school. Within an hour all 50 depositors show up at the bank to demand their $200. The bank can't give them their money.

This happened in the Great Depression during the 1930s when banks loaned money to people to buy houses, cars, boats and other things. As unemployment grew, these people did not have the money to repay the loans. The banks also loaned money to companies, many of which went out of business and didn't repay the banks.

At first the losses were not enough to ruin many banks. Like the Youth Bank, they still made lots of money on other loans. But as rumors spread and people grew worried, they rushed to the banks to withdraw their money. The banks simply didn't have enough cash on hand for all of them. Thus people became frightened and sometimes rioted. Many banks failed and went out of business, causing people to lose their life savings.

Today there is a federally sponsored insurance fund that protects depositors up to a specified amount of a deposit.

Savings and loan associations are simple banks which tend to borrow from people who live nearby. Mostly, too, they lend to nearby people for buying, building, and improving their homes. Every year an extremely high percentage of new homes in America are built with money from local savings and loan associations.

Your local bank may have deposits from a company two thousand miles away, but a savings and loan's deposits are mostly from people who live within its community. A local bank may lend money to people anywhere. It lends money to companies, governments, people all over the country. Some banks lend money around the world, a practice that some people criticize; they maintain that banks should lend most of their money locally to help people who live nearby.

Savings banks are somewhat like savings and loan associations. (And not every state has such banks.) Savings banks tend to borrow and loan money locally, too. They don't offer quite as many services as the "commercial" banks do. For instance, you can't have a checking account in most savings banks throughout the country, though they are starting to be allowed in some areas.

Millions of adults are members of credit unions, which are simple banks, too. They're also like clubs. They borrow money from members (depositors) and lend it to members who want to borrow it. Most credit union loans are for people to buy cars or boats or pay off bills.

Often credit unions are formed for people who work in a company. Some are for villages or towns or parts of a city. My wife and I bought our first house through the credit union of a lodge to which we belonged. We put our savings into its credit union, and when we needed money to buy a house, we borrowed from it. Of course, the money we borrowed was much more than the money we had deposited.

In the course of your life you will hear about all sorts of banks and read about a dozen different kinds of deposits and five dozen types of banking transactions. But the information won't confuse you much if you remember two simple things about banks:

First, they borrow money. The people they borrow from are called depositors, and the amounts of money the banks borrow are called deposits. The bank pays depositors for the use of their money, and what they pay is called interest.

Second, banks lend that money to other people. They may lend it to individuals, to companies, to countries, to organizations of all kinds. They charge interest for the money they lend. The interest on the money they lend is high, while the interest on the money they borrow is low. That leaves extra money, or profit.

Let's recall Mr. Johnson and Mrs. Emery in Chapter One. Each saved $2,000 every year for 30 years. At the end Mr. Johnson had $60,000 for his retirement, while Mrs. Emery had nearly $120,000. Now maybe you can guess why.

Mr. Johnson kept his money in a shoe box. He put $60,000 into that shoe box over the years. He took $60,000 out of it for his retirement.

Mrs. Emery put her savings into a savings account. In other words she loaned it to a bank. The bank paid her different amounts of interest over the years. One year it was high, another year low. The average interest for 30 years was 4%. So if she loaned $60,000 to the bank and it paid 4% for it, she'd earn $2,400, right? (4% × $60,000 = $2,400) *Wrong!* In fact, she earned much more than this!

The first year she deposited $2,000. The bank paid her 4% interest, or $80. (4% × $2,000 = $80) Mrs. Emery left that $80 in the bank. So she started the second year with $2,080. She added her $2,000 savings the second year, making a total of $4,080. The bank that year paid 4% interest on her $4,080. (4% × $4,080 = $163.20.) She left that amount in the bank.

What happened, of course, was the bank paid interest on her interest. She left her interest in the bank as savings. The bank paid interest on it. She left the new interest in the bank, so the bank paid interest on the interest of the first interest.

This is called "compounding." After 30 years Mrs. Emery's savings amounted to $60,000 ($2,000 × 30 years). But the interest she'd left in had "compounded" so much that it was worth *$57,000* after 30 years! Her savings and interest added up to $117,000. What she did made Mr. Johnson's shoe box look silly.

Compounding can be quite dramatic. Suppose you put $1,000 in your local bank when you are 15. You leave it there until you retire at 65. It earns 6% interest per year. You never add anything to it. You simply leave the $1,000 to gather 6% interest. And you leave the interest there to compound.

When you are 50, your savings will have grown to $10,286. When you're 65, it will have swollen to $18,420. If you leave it until you're 80, it will have mushroomed to $44,145! All this from that $1,000 with which you started.

4
CHECK INTO CHECKS

Suppose you have $200 in the Youth Bank at school and Sam wants to borrow it. The Youth Bank is only open for a few hours a day. The only time you can get to it is 8 A.M., but you won't see Sam until 4 P.M. That means you will have to take $200 from the bank in the morning and carry it around all day. But you might be robbed while you're in gym class, or you could lose it. You certainly don't like the idea of carrying $200 with you all day.

So you write a note to the bank. It says, "Please pay Sam Jones my $200 when he gives you this note. You'll know this is from me because I'll sign my name at the bottom. You should ask Sam to show you his student ID card, just to make sure it *is* Sam who presents the note. And make him sign this at the bottom to show that he received the $200."

You give the note to Sam and tell him to collect the money from the Youth Bank whenever he wants it.

The note you've written for Sam is, in effect, a check. It's like the millions of checks that are written in this country every day.

Your check tells your bank to give someone some of your money. If you want to specify who that someone is, like Sam Jones, you write his name on the check. The check then means, "Pay to Sam Jones two hundred dollars. Signed me."

If you don't mind who gets the money, you can write "cash" instead of Sam's name. Then if Sam can't get to the bank either, he can give or "sell" the check to someone else for $200. That other person can take the check to the bank, which will give him your $200.

Sam can even do that with a check which has his name on the front of it. He turns it over and signs his name on the back, just as he would have signed your note. He can give it to the bank that way and receive your $200. Or he can give it to a friend for $200. The friend signs his name under Sam's and gives it to the bank for your $200. When a person signs a check like that, he "endorses" it. His signature is his "endorsement." His endorsement shows the check passed through his hands and he received $200 for it.

Suppose you mail a check for $20 to Sears Roebuck for a portable radio you see in the Sears catalog. How will Sears cash your check? Naturally no one at Sears will have to come to your town, find your bank, endorse the back of your check, and hand it over to the teller.

Sears will endorse your check (with a rubber stamp that says "Sears Roebuck") and give it to the bank in Chicago which handles the company account. *That* bank will give Sears $20 for the check. Then it may pass the check to another bank, which passes it to another—each giving the other $20 for it. When the check finally gets back to your bank, your bank pays $20 to whichever bank handled it last.

To write checks, of course, you have to deposit money in a checking account at the bank. In most places only commercial banks have checking accounts now. Savings and loans, credit unions, and savings banks do not, though this may change in time. After you put money into a checking account, the bank gives you a booklet of checks with your name printed on them. Then when you want to pay for something, you write a check for it.

Probably you've heard someone say, "His check bounced." Here's what that means:

Suppose you give Sam a check for $200, but you only have $150 in your checking account. Sam takes the check to the Youth Bank. The teller refuses it. "We can't give you two hundred dollars for this check, sir. The person who wrote it has only one hundred and fifty dollars here." That means your account is "overdrawn." It means the check will bounce back to you as quickly as Sam can find you. That's why people call checks like this "rubber checks."

Some stores won't accept checks from customers. Too many checks have bounced and left them without money. The store can find the customer, as Sam will find you, but frequently this takes a lot of time. If you are hundreds of miles away, the store will sometimes just rip up the check and accept the loss.

The bank provides quite a service to you when you have a checking account. It safeguards your money, provides you with checks, pays Sam and others who bring in the checks. It sends you a record regularly, showing which checks it has paid for you and how much money you have left.

The bank doesn't pay for all this work. You do.

You pay a small fee for each check. In some banks you pay a monthly fee for the privilege of having a checking account. Sometimes you don't have to pay this if the amount of money you have in the bank remains above—say—$200.

Meanwhile, the bank makes money on whatever money sits in your checking account before you write checks for it. It lends the money, as it lends money you leave in your savings account. It may lend it for 12%. And it makes money because it doesn't pay interest to you for money in your checking account. This may change. Some banks may be allowed to pay interest in the future, and some will let you have a checking account free. Each state and country has its own laws for checking accounts. Your nearest bank will be happy to tell you what they are.

Because they earn no interest on their checking accounts, many people put only a little money in them—only enough to let them write checks for regular bills. All their extra money they lend to a bank. That is, they put it in a *savings* account to earn interest.

If you write several checks that "bounce," Sam—for one—may refuse to accept any more of your checks. Will you have to give him cash?

No. You can still write a check for $200 (if you have that much in the bank). You then ask the bank to write a note to Sam saying that you *do* have $200 in the bank to cover the check. The bank doesn't really write a note. Instead, it stamps the check "CERTIFIED." This is a guarantee to Sam that there is $200 in your account to pay him for this check. When people ask you for a certified check, they are eliminating the chance that your check is no good.

Suppose you travel to Timbuktu and stay at the famous Timbuktu Hotel. When the time comes to pay your hotel bill, you write a check for it. But the hotel clerk refuses the check.

"That's from a bank in Kalamazoo, a long way from here," he tells you. "We don't know if you really have an account there. In fact, we don't even know there *is* a bank there, sir. Do you have any traveler's checks?"

A traveler's check is like a guaranteed check. It is printed by a financial company. You pay a small fee for one (maybe $20.75 for a $20 check) and can usually cash one whether you're in Timbuktu or Kalamazoo.

You can do this because the people at the hotel (or wherever else) know the traveler's check company guarantees its traveler's checks. They don't know if your bank exists. But they *do* know the traveler's check company does. They don't know if you have money in your bank to cover your check. But they *do* know the traveler's check company guarantees to pay them for their traveler's checks.

5

IT'S HERE, THERE, EVERYWHERE

Imagine that you've worked hard, been lucky, and Sam paid back that $200. Now, believe it or not, you have $500!

Your friend Sally, who never runs out of ideas, comes to see you. She says she has three boys working her newspaper route for her. She pays them 4½¢ per paper while the newspaper company pays her 6¢ per paper. Thus she makes 1½¢ on each paper by doing nothing more than organizing the boys.

"You're not so crazy, Sally," you tell her.

"Thanks, pal. Here's my latest idea. I'm going to grow vegetables and flowers this summer and sell them at a little stand."

Sally explains that she's going to grow her products on an empty lot. In fact, she's going to *buy* the lot. She can get it for a song—only $500. And she wants to do it with *your* $500, which she'd like to borrow for five years—at interest, of course.

You think about it overnight, and when you see Sally the next day she offers to pay 8% interest on your loan for the next five years. Still you are wary, and she grows angry.

"What do you want?" she cries. "A guarantee written in

blood? Do you want my clothes if the vegetables don't grow? Do you want my land and the roadside stand if I don't make the payments?" She pauses, realizing she has said something interesting. "Hmmm . . . my land and my stand if I don't make the payments?"

You offer to settle for that, and you both think about it for a few days. She returns with some questions. "Okay, suppose I agree to that? But what if I don't pay? What if I don't make the payments and you take my land? What will you do with it?"

"I'd sell it to get my money back."

Sally says, "That makes sense. But what if this happened after four years? What if I'd paid most of your money back by the time it happened? That doesn't sound fair. You'd be collecting double the money."

"You're right," you agree. "It's not fair. Okay, if that happens, I'll just keep what you owe me. You can have the rest. If you only owe me a hundred and I sell it for five hundred, I'll give you the extra four hundred. That's fair."

What you've just done is agree to a mortgage with Sally. You've heard the word "mortgage" before and you probably thought it was more complicated than that. But it's not.

A mortgage is a loan *against some property*. You've now loaned money against Sally's property—her land and stand.

This happens in a mortgage: Someone says here's what property I've got. How much will you lend me on it? That's virtually what Sally did.

If you think you might lend money against a property, what should you do beforehand?

Suppose you have $50,000 in the bank, and suppose Sally wants to borrow all of it. She wants you to mortgage her plot and vegetable stand for the $50,000. If she can't pay you back, you can take over the property and sell it.

But this raises a vital question: Is that property worth $50,000? If Sally can't repay and you try to sell the property, no buyer will *pay* $50,000 for it. So you'll lose money. Therefore, you must determine how much that plot is worth.

Organizations that grant mortgages have people who do nothing but this. Their job is to value property for the bank or whoever is going to grant a mortgage.

Suppose Sally asks a bank for the $500 mortgage. The bank sends its valuer (or appraiser) to look at her land. He determines a few things. First, he learns that the property next to hers was sold for only $400 last year. And he feels that too few cars pass by there to provide many customers for her stand. So he tells his bank the property is only worth $450. He suggests a loan of only $375 against it.

Next, Sally tries her nearest savings and loan association for a mortgage. It sends its valuer to the property. He finds out that property across the street sold for $750 last month. He also learns that the streets around there are going to be changed in two months. When they are, the traffic on Sally's street will double. So he tells the savings and loan that her property is worth $700 to $900. He feels a $500 loan will be safe. If Sally can't make the payments, he feels the savings and loan should easily be able to sell it for at least the $500.

Your house may be mortgaged. If it is a rented house, the landlord may have a mortgage on it from his bank. If you live in an apartment house, it is probably mortgaged. *Your school* may have a mortgage, with some of the school taxes going each year to pay off the mortgage. *Your church* probably has a mortgage. Your theatre, too. Your television and radio stations are likely to be mortgaged—at least their buildings are. The farms and orchards that provide your food have mortgages. Even the stadium where your favorite team plays is probably mortgaged.

Why so many mortgages? Sally knows the answer. The man from whom she is buying the land wants the $500 pronto. He happens to be an old man and he wants to enjoy the money *now*.

The building company that constructs your house wants its money now, too. It has to pay for the timber and windows and other materials now. It has to pay its carpenters every week.

Mortgages are popular because people want to buy property. They want to buy or build houses and apartments and shopping centers, which usually cost more money than the people have.

A young couple, for instance, wants to buy a $35,000 home for their growing family. If they have to save that much first, they will need 20 years to do so. Their children will be grown and gone from home by the time the couple have enough money for the house. So they resort to a mortgage. They turn to someone, or some firm, that already has $35,000. They ask to borrow it, to use it to pay for the house. They pay it back, along with interest, over several years. That's a mortgage.

By now you should know where to turn for a $35,000 mortgage. What sort of firms amass large amounts of money for lending? Banks and savings and loans, of course. Remember, they borrow money from depositors and pay them low interest. Then they loan the money to other people at high interest rates. Much of what they loan is in the form of mortgages.

In some countries insurance companies lend money in mortgages. Sometimes wealthy individuals do so. Some companies will mortgage houses for their most valuable employees, making it easy for the employee to buy a house.

The man who is selling Sally his land is old and wants his $500 now. But if he were a young person he might let Sally pay the $500 over several years. In other words, he could lend her the money under a mortgage agreement. He could mortgage his own property. This is often done by an individual, and there are a couple of good reasons for it.

One is that the person is anxious to sell the property and doesn't want to wait for Sally to persuade a bank to lend money to her. Since that could take a long time, he agrees to lend the money to her himself.

The other reason is that some sellers want to have money dribbling in for the next 20 years and agree to mortgages for that many years. Many small businesses are sold in this way. For example, a grocer will work in his own business until he's ready to retire. Then he sells it to a young person for $150,000. The young person gives the grocer $30,000 in cash, say, and borrows the remaining $120,000 from the grocer at 8% per year. In paying this off, he pays the grocer several thousand dollars per year for 25 years. The grocer retires in Florida. He takes care of his living expenses with the payments that come from the man who bought the store.

That $30,000 cash the grocer asked for is called a down payment. A mortgager normally asks for a down payment because he thinks this way: You want to borrow $150,000 from me to buy my $150,000 store, but suppose you then fail to make the payments? If I had to take the store over, you've hardly lost any money because I will have provided all the money.

But suppose you have to make a $30,000 down payment from your own savings? Then the mortgage money from me will be only $120,000. My risk will be less. It will be $30,000 less. And now you will stand to lose your $30,000 down payment if you fail to make payments. Maybe you'll work harder to make the store successful if you have $30,000 at stake.

Some people apply for an FHA or a VA mortgage. FHA is the Federal Housing Administration; VA is the Veterans Administration. They were formed to help people get mortgages to buy homes. Organizations like these usually won't lend money themselves, but they will tell a bank that if the person can't make the necessary payments, the organization will.

Interest rates go up and down in mortgages. One may get a mortgage today at 8% and in three months have to pay 8¼% or 7¾%.

Once upon a time, the interest rate didn't change on a mortgage. If you lent Sally $500 at 8%, she would pay 8% from the first payment to the last. Today, however, mortgagers are getting the right to raise and lower interest rates during the mortgage period. For instance, you could have Sally pay higher or lower interest each year—going by whatever your local bank was charging each year.

Interest rates go up and down for a basically simple reason. When the lenders (banks, etc.) have more money than people want to borrow, they lower the interest to make their money more attractive. When they don't have enough money to go around, they raise the interest rates.

Now the difference between ¼% and ½% probably may not seem like much to you. But it's more than you suspect. Let's study Sally's mortgage with you on the basis that she has borrowed $500 at 8% per year and is going to pay you $110 per year.

IT'S HERE, THERE, EVERYWHERE

Year 1	Sally owes	$500	
	Plus 8% interest	40	
		$540	
	She pays	110	
	That leaves	$430	still owed to you.
Year 2	Sally owes	$430.00	
	Plus 8% interest	34.40*	
		$464.40	
	She pays	110.40	
	That leaves	$354.00	
Year 3	Sally owes	$354.00	
	Plus 8% interest	28.32	
		$382.32	
	She pays	110.32	
	That leaves	$272.00	
Year 4	Sally owes	$272.00	
	Plus 8% interest	.21.76	
		$293.76	
	She pays	110.76	
	That leaves	$183.00	
Year 5	Sally owes	$183.00	
	Plus 8%	14.64	
		$197.64	
	She pays	110.64	
	That leaves	$ 87.00	
Year 6	Sally owes	$ 87.00	
	Plus 8%	6.96	
		$ 93.96	
	She pays	93.96	

*Notice the 8% interest is refigured every year. Sally pays 8% interest per year. After one year she still has $430 of yours. So that money earns another 8% interest.

Sally borrowed $500 from you. But her total payments to you are $646.08. The interest came to $146.08. She needed 6 years to pay back your money at $110.00 per year.

Now, let's raise Sally's interest only ½% more per year. Before you look at the answer, guess how much more Sally will pay you.

She has $500 at 8½% She pays you $110 per year.

Year 1	Sally owes	$500.00
	Plus 8½% interest	42.50
		$542.50
	She pays	110.00
	That leaves	$432.50 still owed to you
Year 2	Sally owes	$432.50
	Plus 8½% interest	36.76
		$469.26
	She pays	110.26
	That leaves	$359.00
Year 3	Sally owes	$359.00
	Plus 8½% interest	30.52
		$389.52
	She pays	110.52
	That leaves	$279.00
Year 4	Sally owes	$279.00
	Plus 8½% interest	23.72
		$302.72
	She pays	110.72
	That leaves	$192.00
Year 5	Sally owes	$192.00
	Plus 8½% interest	16.32
		$208.32
	She pays	110.32
	That leaves	$ 98.00
Year 6	Sally owes	$ 98.00
	Plus 8½% interest	8.33
		$106.33
	She pays	106.33

IT'S HERE, THERE, EVERYWHERE

Her total payments to you are $658.15. The loan was for $500. So the interest amounted to $158.15.

That ½% meant $12 more in payments. And that was only over 6 years.

If this was a 20-year mortgage for $20,000, the difference in ½% would be several thousand dollars. Thus it pays for everyone to shop around for his or her mortgage. The savings and loan may lend at 8% while the bank lends at 8½% now. By the time a person pays back the money, he's saved several thousand dollars.

By this time you probably know the answers to the riddles about Mr. Johnson, Mrs. Emery, and Amy Brown. All bought homes with prices of $25,000. But each paid a different amount for them. Why?

Mr. Johnson wrote a check for $25,000 and bought his house. That sale was complete, then and there, for $25,000.

Mrs. Emery only had $10,000 in cash. She used that as a down payment. She borrowed the remaining $15,000 from her bank as a mortgage. She paid 7½% interest on that money. She made payments to the bank of $1,400 per year for 23 years.

Like Sally, she ended up paying a lot more than the money she borrowed. She had to pay lots of interest over the years. In fact, her total payments in 23 years amounted to $32,000. Now add that to her $10,000 down payment. She paid $42,000 for her $25,000 apartment. Or you can say she paid $25,000 for her $25,000 apartment. And she paid $17,000 interest to a bank for borrowing $15,000 for 23 years.

Amy was in the same fix as Mrs. Emery, only worse. She had only $5,000 for a down payment. She had to borrow $20,000 on a mortgage. She took 25 years to pay it back. The 7½% interest over those years came to $25,000. So she paid back $45,000 ($20,000 she borrowed plus $25,000 interest). And she paid $5,000 as a down payment. That totals $50,000 for her $25,000 home. Let's spell it out more clearly:

Mr. Johnson

Paid at Start	Money Borrowed and Paid Back	Interest Paid on the Borrowed Money
$25,000	$0	$0

Total $25,000

Mrs. Emery

Paid at Start	Money borrowed and Paid Back	Interest Paid on the Borrowed Money
$10,000	$15,000	$17,000

Total $42,000

Amy Brown

Paid at Start	Money borrowed and Paid Back	Interest Paid on the Borrowed Money
$5,000	$20,000	$25,000

Total $50,000

The $500 loan you gave Sally is a first mortgage. Nobody else is loaning her money against the vegetable property. You are the first lender, so yours is called a first mortgage.

Suppose Sally goes to Sam and asks for a $100 loan. Sam says okay, but he wants to mortgage her vegetable plot. She tells him it's already mortgaged.

He *can* take a second mortgage against her property for his $100. That means he stands in line behind you. If she can't pay, you sell the property. This is how you get your money back. But what can Sam do? He is entitled to money left after you take yours. So he's taking a bigger risk than you. Let's say Sally can't make even the first payment. You can sell the property for only $500 and recover all your money. Only if you sell it for $600 will Sam get his back.

Sally can turn to someone else for a *third* mortgage. That would be an outright gamble for the mortgager, who stands in line behind Sam.

Now if Sam takes a second mortgage, he takes a bigger risk than you. So he deserves a reward for taking a greater risk. Of course the greater the risk, the greater the interest, and so Sam will probably charge 12% interest for his second mortgage loan. And since the third mortgage is a much greater risk, it probably will have an interest rate of 15% to 20%.

Lots of people buy houses or businesses with a first and second mortgage. They borrow, say, $30,000 from a bank for 20 years at 8%, which is their first mortgage. Then they borrow, say, $3,000 from a friend for 4 years at 11%, which is their second mortgage.

Often the first mortgager tells the borrower NO SECOND MORTGAGES because it doesn't want the borrower struggling too much to make payments.

My wife and I bought our first house with three mortgages. The first was from a society to which I belonged. It was for 25 years at 7½%. The second was from my mother-in-law. It was a much smaller amount, for 5 years at 10%. The third was from my father-in-law. It was for about $1,000, for 2 years at 12%.

We had to make a payment every month on all three mortgages. I worked day and night for a while to make enough money. It was worth it, though, to have a good home for our children.

People do some interesting things with mortgages. Let's look at Sally again, who is going to end up with three properties here and barely spend any money.

First she gets a $500 first mortgage from you for the vegetable plot she buys. She gets a $100 second mortgage from Sam. (Even though she only paid $500 for the land.) That takes care of one property.

Next, she buys Mr. Porcorelli's big strawberry beds. He's too old to work in them anymore. She knows she can sell the berries at her stand. He wants $1,000 for the strawberry beds. Sally says she has only $100 cash, Sam's cash. Mr. Porcorelli takes a $900 mortgage for the remainder.

Then she buys another piece of land across the street for more vegetables. She pays $1,000 for the land. The Youth Bank gives her an $800 mortgage. She draws $200 from her savings to make the $1,000.

After all this, people will think Sally is pretty prosperous. She "owns" three plots of land and a vegetable stand. She must have a lot of money to own so much land at her age. But, as you know, she only has $200 invested! For her $500 piece of land, she received $600 in mortgage money from you and Sam. She didn't spend any of her own money for it. And she ended up with $100 extra from Sam.

Then she used Sam's $100 as down payment on Mr. Porcorelli's $1,000 lot.

And she put $200 down on the $1,000 land the Youth Bank mortgaged.

Now she owns land worth $2,500, but so far she's only parted with $200 out of her own pocket. Clever! Of course, she has one big worry now. She must make enough money from vegetables and berries to pay off all the mortgages. Three mortgages add up to a lot of potatoes.

6

TWO'S COMPANY

Sam is a roaring success these days because he publishes a neighborhood newspaper. He bought an old mimeograph machine to print it, hired some reporters to gather news, and sells advertisements to nearby stores.

One day he shows up on your doorstep. "Need your help, old pal."

"Don't tell me you want more money! You've got all the money now. I should borrow from you!"

"No, I don't need money. I need a partner."

You eye Sam warily. "Partner? What for?"

"I want to get bigger. I want to put out another six papers."

"Holy mackerel! Six more? That's a pretty big job, Sam."

"That's why I'm talking to you, dummy. I need a partner to help create another six papers. We can build a newspaper empire. Imagine! We can split all the money we make."

You and Sam discuss the problem for days. The need is for money, and mortgages are out of the question. You don't own any land on which a bank can take a mortgage; a bank won't take a mortgage on a pile of paper and seven mimeograph machines. Finally you and Sam begin to talk about forming a company.

What is a company, anyway? Why do people form them?

A company is like an enormous pie. It is cut into hundreds of pieces. Pieces are called stocks, or shares. When the company is formed, some or all of these pieces are sold to people. This is how the company gets the money with which to start. It *sells* pieces of itself. The pieces are called stock. The people who buy them are called stockholders. They hold the stock.

There you have one reason why people form companies. They want to raise money to use in a business. So they sell shares of their company. Another reason is that a company protects its owners and shields them to an extent.

Let's say you own a business which is *not* a company. It's just a grocery store. And let's say the store goes broke, owing thousands of dollars. The people to whom it owes money can come to you to collect it because you own the business. They can make you sell your house and car or motorbike to pay them. After all, you own the business and are liable for its debts.

But let's say the grocery is a *company* in which you own most of the stock. If the company goes broke, the people to whom it owes money *cannot* make you sell your house. You are *not* liable for the company's debts. In the eyes of the law, the company is like a separate person, liable for its own bills. Your liability is *limited* to whatever money you paid the company for the stock.

That is why companies in Canada, England, Australia, New

Zealand, and other places have the word "Limited" or "Ltd." after them. It means that stockholders are shielded, not liable for the company's debts. Their liability is limited.

Finally making Sam understand, you set about forming a company. You decide to slice the company into 100 equal shares, called stocks, each worth $20.

Sam will buy 10 shares. That will give the company $200. You will buy 10 shares. That will give the company another $200. You plan to sell 30 more shares to people you know. That will bring in another $600.

So the company will have $1,000 with which to start and have another 50 shares in reserve which it can sell in the future when it needs more money.

You and Sam agree that stockholders must share in the profits. "We'll take some profits every year and divvy them up. If there are fifty shares, we'll divide the profit fifty ways. There'll be so much profit for each share."

"Hey, that isn't fair! You and I will be doing all the work, but the stockholders won't be doing anything."

"Well, then, let's have the company employ us. It can pay us each a salary for our work. Then we'll get a share of the profits on top of our salary."

This is exactly what companies do. They sell shares of stock, which provide the money to operate. They then set aside part of their profits each year and divide them so that each share of stock earns a share of the profits. Each piece of profit is called a dividend. The profit is *divided* into dividends. You and Sam would say it's "divvyed" up.

Meanwhile companies pay salaries to their employees. Some

employees also own shares of stock. So they receive salaries for their work and dividends for their gamble. For owning stock is a gamble. A company can fail, and you take a risk when you own its stock and should be rewarded for your risk. You deserve a dividend.

When you start to sell stock in your company, old Mr. Porcorelli likes the idea but has a few tricky requests.

"How is a stockholder to know if you're doing well or poorly? I'll be retired in Florida. Every year I'd like a report. Tell me how much the company owes. How much other people owe the company. Tell me how many papers you're selling. Things like that. And I want some people to represent us stockholders. I'm not too smart when it comes to business. These guys would be. They'd keep an eye on you, meet with you once in a while. Ask how the company's doing. And you'd have to ask their permission to do something big, like buying a building."

"We'd have to get their permission?"

"Sure. They would represent the stockholders. And the stockholders own the company. So before the company does anything big, it should check with the stockholders to make sure it's okay with them. It's not always easy to get in touch with every stockholder. So you just check with our representatives. And they should agree on the dividend each year, too."

"Why?"

"Because the company shouldn't give all its profits out every year. It should hold some back. It might need that money during the year. Things might get tough. It might need some money in a hurry. If it hands it all out to the stockholders for dividends, it can't very well ask for it back. Also sometimes a company tries to be stingy. It doesn't want to give any dividends to the stockholders. Our representatives will make sure that doesn't happen, too."

"Fair enough. What do you call these representatives?"

"Directors. I call them company directors."

That *is* how companies operate. They issue an annual report to their stockholders; many send a report every three months.

Company directors meet regularly, as the "board of directors." They have a leader, a chairman, which is the origin of the expression "chairman of the board."

The directors are supposed to represent the stockholders. If the company does poorly, they will take some action to protect the stockholders' investment. For instance, they will sometimes fire the top executives of a company and hire others. The directors approve the dividend and approve or disapprove major actions of the company.

The directors are elected by the stockholders. The election in large companies is usually cut and dried, however. Most stockholders never come to the annual meeting when the election takes place.

Only a fraction of stockholders come to an annual meeting. A large company may have 500,000 stockholders, and a person who owns only 100 shares in such a company won't make much impact at an annual meeting. Directors are usually businessmen. They know a lot about how companies work and, by looking at the facts and figures, can tell if a company is sick or healthy.

In large companies, directors are usually well known in the business world. This is important because it gives stockholders confidence. Some people are professional directors who sit on the boards of dozens of companies and are steeped in a knowledge of business.

So you form the company and sell the shares to people you know. The stockholders elect a board of directors, and the company starts several more newspapers which are popular. In its first year the company makes a $200 profit.

You and Sam recommend to the directors that a dividend of $2 be paid on each share of stock. A month later Mr. Porcorelli dies in Florida, and Mrs. Porcorelli inherits his stock in your company. Knowing nothing of business, she wants to sell the shares to her brother so that she'll have money to pay for her husband's funeral.

Of course she can sell the shares. But how much should she charge? Mr. Porcorelli paid $20 for each one, but that was 18 months ago, when the company was first starting. It wasn't making any money then, but now it's making a good profit and paying dividends. Aren't the shares worth more now than when Mr. Porcorelli bought them?

The answer is yes. They probably are worth more money now, though how much more is hard to say. You could add up everything the company owns, then subtract all the bills it owes. That would tell you what the company is worth. Now divide that by the number of shares. That will tell you what each share is worth —on paper.

What people will pay for them, however, is a different matter. Let's imagine two situations.

Situation No. 1:

"What do you think of that little newspaper company?"

"That one the teenagers run? Terrible. My sister says her papers are always late and have lots of mistakes in them. And you know Johnson's Grocery? They stopped advertising in the paper. Never again. Kids ran their ad upside down two weeks in a row. Besides, their office looks dumpy, like maybe they're losing money. And that kid, Sam, I hear he's not the brightest student. And he borrows a lot of money around the place. And that other kid, the one he pals around with!"

"So you don't think I should buy stock in their company?"

"Stock? Heavens, no! At least I wouldn't pay much for it. It seems risky to me."

Situation No. 2:

"What do you know about that little newspaper company?"

"The one the teenagers run? It's okay in my book. Everybody I've talked to says they make good little newspapers and their delivery system can't be beat. And Johnson's Grocery swears by them. One week they ran their ad upside down by mistake. They ran the ad for free for the next three weeks to make up for it. Their offices are spotless. The whole outfit looks like it's making money. And that kid, Sam, he's on the high honor roll at school. Good little businessman, too."

"So you think I'd be smart to buy stock in the company?"

"Not a bad idea. I don't know how much you'll have to pay, but it's probably a good stake in the future. I think it'll grow more valuable. That company's on the way up, if you ask me."

Situations like this cause stocks to go up and down in value. Even stocks of big companies like General Motors and Kodak are affected in this way.

First of all, people look at the facts, of course. Does the company make profits? Does it pay healthy dividends every year? Or has it skipped dividends some years?

Secondly, people look at other things about the company. Does it make good products? Does it have the best people working for it? (Big companies have hired astronauts because people trust them and think more highly of the companies.) Does the company have many labor problems, many strikes? Is it a popular company? Does it have a good name?

It won't help if the company was caught giving a bribe to a government official. It won't help if people read that the company's factories pollute rivers and lakes. It won't help if the company makes products that are becoming old-fashioned.

People think about other matters before they buy any stocks. Let's eavesdrop on yet another conversation.

Situation No. 3:

"I've got a chance to buy some stock in that teenage newspaper company. I don't know if I will, though."

"I don't blame you. The way this country's going, I wouldn't invest a nickel in the safest company in the world. Not this year."

"Neither would I. Unemployment is going up and up. Prices are going up like rockets. I may be out of work soon myself. I don't feel like gambling on any stocks this year."

"You're smart. I had some money in stocks. But I sold 'em a couple of months ago while the going was good. Put my money in the bank where it's safe."

"Good move, good move."

In other words, people's confidence has a lot to do with the value of all stocks. When people are afraid of the future, stock prices come down all over the country. When people are afraid, they put more of their money in banks and shoe toes. Stock prices come down. When people feel good about the future, they invest more in stocks. Stock prices go up.

Another thing that affects stock prices is the amount of money available. Suppose ten small companies started in your community at the same time yours did. Suppose they all tried to sell their shares when you sold yours. There's only so much money to go around in your community. If you managed to sell yours, you'd probably have to settle for less than $20 per share.

A country is no different. There is only so much money, and too much may go into new stocks. Or too much may go to the banks because they raise their interest rates. Or too much of it may go for food and clothing because prices have shot upward. This leaves less money for people to invest in stocks and causes stock prices to go down. On the other hand, if there is a lot of extra money around, stock prices are likely to go up.

Suppose Mrs. Porcorelli has some other company shares to sell, like shares from Kodak which neither her brother nor sister wants to buy. She phones her best friend. "Are you crazy, Bertha?" is the answer. "You know Frank's out of work." She writes to her cousins. They're broke, as usual.

Suppose 200,000 people like Mrs. Porcorelli have shares to sell today. And 200,000 more have shares to sell tomorrow. They all start phoning friends. And suppose 200,000 people decide today they want to buy some shares. They phone and write to relatives to ask if they have shares to sell. Only the phone companies and post office would be happy with this situation.

These people need a place to buy and sell shares of stock. They need a marketplace. And they have one. It's called a stock market, or stock exchange.

If you are in America, you may hear about the famous New York Stock Exchange. Or the American Stock Exchange. If you are in Canada, you hear about the Toronto and Montreal Stock Exchanges. Then there is the world-famous London Stock Exchange which started in 1773. There are stock exchanges the world over, in Tokyo, Johannesburg, Frankfurt, Brussels, Sydney, Paris, Zurich, and many more cities.

A stock exchange is a market. It has "members" who are somewhat like storekeepers in a market. They don't actually buy and own shares, then turn around and sell them, as storekeepers do with their goods. Instead they buy shares *for* you and sell *for* you. You pay them a fee for doing the buying and selling *for* you.

You contact a member of the stock exchange and say, "I've got a thousand shares of Kodak. Will you please sell them for me tomorrow? I want twenty-two dollars each for them."

"I'll try," he promises. "But today people won't pay more than twenty-one dollars for them. Maybe they'll pay twenty-two tomorrow."

"If they don't, you can sell them at twenty-one dollars," you direct him.

He sells them and you send your stock certificates to him. He gets them to the person who buys them and sends you the money they paid—after he takes out his fee.

In a big market like the New York Stock Exchange you wouldn't phone the member, of course. If you and all his customers called him, he'd be on the phone all day. Instead, you phone a nearby office of his company and that office tells the New York office what you want to do. The New York office contacts its man who is working at the Exchange, telling him to sell 1,000 Kodak shares at $21 or $22.

You'll recall that Amy Brown bought a part of the Columbia Broadcasting System. CBS is a company that has millions of shares of stock, and when it makes profits it pays a dividend on each share. Like Amy, you can buy a piece of CBS—or Coca-

Cola, Pepsi Cola, or almost any large company. Shares are normally sold 100 in a bunch, or a "lot." That may be too much money for a start, but some exchange members will handle "odd lots," which means a few shares at a time. Ask your local stock broker about this if you're interested.

Your Me n' Sam Newspaper Company shares won't be sold on the big stock exchanges for a while—if ever. The company will have to be worth many millions of dollars first. Otherwise nobody in the exchange will know anything about your company. And if nobody there knows your company, they wouldn't want to buy and sell your shares. Meantime your shares of stock will be bought and sold privately, as is the stock of most small companies.

If you have some shares in the stock market, how do you know what they are worth every day? If you phone your stock broker every day to find out, he'll get tired of you pretty quickly.

You look in the newspaper. Most papers have a list of popular stocks which tells you what prices each stock sold for that day—the highest price and the lowest price.

Perhaps you own shares in only two companies. But you will want to know how other shares are going, too. If most stocks are going down, it will tell you that people are losing confidence. Or it will tell you that there isn't as much money around as there was. This may affect the prices of your stocks eventually, so you'll be keen to know how other stocks are doing.

If you tried to keep track of every stock listed in the paper, it might take hours every night—if your paper lists a lot of stocks. There is an easier way. Some people pick a number of key stocks and keep track of them. They lump the prices of each of these stocks together for a certain day and get an average price—say 500. They do the same tomorrow and get 503. The next day the average is 506.

This probably means that most shares are going up. It's like your history teacher saying that the class average on tests is five points higher now than it was last semester. It doesn't mean that every student raised his mark, but that most of them probably did.

You can learn what the stock *averages* are every day. You can read them in the paper, hear them on the radio, see them on television. The best known one in America is the Dow Jones Average. There are several different averages for different exchanges around the world. Some averages come from lumping together *all* of the stocks sold on a particular exchange, not just key stocks. Each average has its own fans and its own critics.

This is a good place to ask, "How do we know the true value of stock?" The answer depends on when you ask that question.

When a company issues stock, its value is what the company says it is. The company says, "We will buy this building and these materials and make a thousand of these products with the money that comes from the shares. All of this will be worth $100,000. Since we are issuing 1,000 shares, each one will be worth $100. That's the price at which we are selling them." (If the company grossly overprices its stock, no one will buy the shares.)

A year later when the stock is in the marketplace, its value is what investors say it is. No matter what the company's assets are, no matter what its stock should be worth according to business textbooks—if people don't like it, they won't pay that much. If they worry about the economy, if they run low on money—they won't pay that much.

Here's an extreme example: The Jones Company is worth $1,000,000 on paper. Its factories and other assets are worth that much easily, and it is making a good profit every year. On paper its stock should be worth $30 per share.

But the Jones factory is found to be sitting on an earthquake fault that scientists say will cause disaster within ten years. To make matters worse, the factory is in a tiny country that is at war with a large country—and is losing. And Jones Company's only product is a hazardous pesticide which most countries say they will outlaw in a few years. Not many investors will sink $30 into Jones Company shares.

Sam comes to you one day and says, "We need more money—a lot of money." There are five newspapers for sale, and you agree you'd like to buy them.

"We could sell the shares," you suggest. "Remember the fifty we still have. We started with one hundred shares, but we sold only fifty shares at the beginning."

You and Sam agree to give the company stockholders first crack at the shares.

Many big companies have shares that have never been issued. They hold them off the market until they need more money. If the company is doing well, they can someday sell them at a high price. It is common practice for companies to offer these shares to the people who own their stock now. The directors have to approve such things, naturally.

Sam comes to you again a year later and says it's time to start a magazine. More money is needed, but all those leftover shares have been sold. What now?

Sam has an idea: "Couldn't we just run off some more shares and sell 'em around the place?"

In fact, Sam's right. If the directors approve, you can issue more stock and raise more money. You must be careful, though. If you issue another 100 shares right now, you will lessen the value of the 100 shares already out. Your profit this year will have to be spread over 200 shares instead of 100 shares. It will probably mean less dividend per share. So the shares won't be as valuable to the owners.

You will be smart if you issue only 20 new shares. You might even announce that the company won't pay a dividend on the new shares for the first year. Big companies issue new shares every day.

Let's say your company owns 30 of its own shares, which is legal. A company can buy them from stockholders, and you already know that a company may hold stock that has not been issued yet.

Sam wants to buy another newspaper worth $600 or $700. The newspaper has 100 shares of stock currently selling for $6 a share.

"Let's offer those stockholders seven dollars for each share," Sam suggests. "They'll make extra money if they sell to us."

"That means we have to have some cash to pay for them," you say. "We'll have to sell some of our thirty shares, right?"

"I guess so."

"Do you suppose, Sam, we could swap with them? I mean our

stock for theirs? Let's not sell our stock for money to buy theirs. Instead let's just offer their stockholders some of our *shares* for theirs. I mean the company would do this. It has thirty shares to offer."

"But our shares are worth thirty dollars. Theirs are only worth six, maybe seven at the most."

"Okay. Let's offer them one of our shares for four of theirs. That's a good deal. If one of their stockholders has four shares, they're worth about twenty-four dollars, right? Six dollars apiece. He swaps these for one of ours. Now he has one share worth thirty dollars."

"And he has one share of a bigger company that is really making money."

"Right!"

"Well, how many of their shares do we want?"

"All we need is fifty-one out of the hundred. That will give us a majority at the stockholders' meeting. When we have a majority, we can elect our own directors. And our directors will have us run the paper. Our company will control that company."

This sort of thing takes place every week. It's called a takeover. A big company will take over a small company by buying its stock at the stock exchange until it has 51%. Then it has control of the other company.

It may not be easy to buy all the stock at the stock exchange. There may be too many shares all over the country for the big company to get its hands on. Besides, word soon gets out that the big company wants to buy these shares. When stockholders know this, they ask higher and higher prices for their stock.

So usually a big company takes a shortcut. It writes to all the stockholders of the small company. "We will give you seven dollars for each of your shares. Are you interested?"

The directors of the small company may approve and write to the stockholders: "Take the deal. It's a good one." Or they may disapprove: "Hold out for more money," they advise. Or, "Don't sell. Your company is making lots of money on its own. You will make bigger dividends if you keep your stock."

The stockholders are free to do what they want. If enough of them sell so that the big company gets 51% of the shares, it has control of the small company.

Now you know why it's healthy for your company to pay dividends each year, publish a good annual report, and look prosperous. Such things keep your stock popular and your stock prices high. If you want to buy another company by using your stock, you can buy more when your stock is high priced.

Suppose your stock price slumped to $15. You would have to trade one share for only two of the shares of the other newspaper. In order to get 52 of their shares, you would have to trade 26 of yours. As it was, you only had to trade 13 shares. That's because your shares were worth so much.

Have you ever heard of *preferential* treatment? It means special treatment. There are some shares of stock that get special treatment and are called "preferred stocks." (Until now we've only talked about "common stocks.") Companies usually have only a few preferred stocks compared with their common stock.

Preferred stocks usually cost more. They are worth more because they usually have a fixed dividend. That is, they are supposed to earn, say, a $2 dividend every year. They get preferential treatment. Suppose the company only makes a small profit. First the preferred stocks take their $2 dividend. If there is any profit left over, the common stock will have a dividend. It has to stand in line behind the preferred stock.

Actually there are several different types of stocks. Some have extra voting power. However, common stock is by far the most popular in most companies.

Companies often split stock to keep it manageable.

Suppose your company grows so valuable its stock is worth $300 per share. Stockholders can't find buyers for their stock because the price is too high for most people. You make it easier by calling in each share of stock and issuing, say, three in its place. In other words, you "split" your stock into three. Each new share will be worth $100 and be easier to trade than the old ones were.

Most companies try to keep their stocks in the $30 to $60 range, within reach of the average investor. Stock is normally bought and sold in lots of 100 shares. If a stock rises to $100, a hundred shares will cost $10,000. That's too much for most investors.

Companies split stock in the other direction, too. It's called splitting, but ought to be called lumping. If a company's stock is worth only $2 per share, some investors will think the company can't amount to much. Mr. Porcorelli might have thought this if you had issued a thousand $2 shares instead of a hundred $20 shares.

A company remedies this by calling in lots of, say, ten shares and issuing one share in return. The value of the company doesn't change. But the value of each share will now be $20 instead of $2. This makes it more impressive.

You can form a company almost as easily as we made it sound earlier. Each country and state has different laws, but the following apply in most places: You need at least three people to do the incorporating, and each one pledges to buy so many shares. Usually one has to be a resident of the country, sometimes of the state. And often one has to pay a tax to incorporate.

You fill out an application with the company name, its purpose, the names and addresses of the incorporators. You reveal how much stock you are authorizing. Then you file this with the Secretary of State of your state, or a similar officer if you don't live in a state. He may check you out to see that what you say in the form is true. He will check to see that your company name is not the same as another company's. When he approves your application, your organization becomes a company.

7

GAMBLING

Example No. 1:
　One day you and Sam visit a farmer to write a story about him for your papers. He grows carrots and tells you he's worried because he's not sure he can sell all his carrots at a decent price this year.
　"What's a decent price?" asks Sam.
　"Oh, probably twenty cents a pound."
　"We'll take five hundred pounds if you'll deliver them next week."
　You're astounded. "Sam! What do you mean *we*? I don't want any!"
　Sam signals you to shut up. After you leave the farmer, Sam stops at a phone booth and calls Sally.
　"Remember, Sally, you told me how expensive carrots were getting? How would you like five hundred pounds of the most

beautiful carrots for only twenty-five cents a pound? You would? Great! We'll deliver them next week."

What Sam has done was to buy a commodity—carrots—at a price and sell at a higher price. He and the seller and the buyer are all happy.

Nevertheless Sam undertook a real gamble. Sally might not have wanted to buy carrots at 25¢ or any price. He might not have found anybody to buy them for even 20¢. Sam might have had more carrots on his hands than he could eat in a lifetime.

Example No. 2:

You and Sam return to the farmer in the spring and Sam asks, "How would you like it if I bought your carrots this year before you even plant them?"

"You're a crazy kid," the farmer says. "I like your ideas, but you're crazy."

"No, I'm not," Sam says. "I know you're going to grow carrots. I know you're going to worry about whether you can sell them. All that worry is bad for your ulcers. I can take all your worries away. I'll sign a contract with you now. When your carrots are ripe, I'll take them for eighteen cents a pound. That's a guaranteed price. I'll put it in writing now."

The farmer agrees. "I know that by the time they're ripe I may be able to sell them for twenty-five cents a pound," he says. "On the other hand, the best price by then may be only twelve cents a pound. It's a gamble. The future is a gamble. If I sign with you, I have no gamble. It's a deal."

Sam keeps quiet until summer. Then he calls on Sally.

"Sal, how much are you paying for carrots now?"

"Oh, Sam, it's ridiculous. I have to pay forty cents a pound. I can't believe how high the price is."

"How would you like some at thirty-five cents?"

"Hey, if they're good carrots I'll take 'em. Wow! Thirty-five cents! I save five cents a pound. Good deal."

Here the farmer sold Sam the "future"—his future carrot crop. Sam held onto the "future." When the carrots ripened, he sold the "future" and made a huge profit.

The gamble, was, of course, that by summer the price Sally paid for carrots might have been 16¢. Sam would have had to buy carrots at 18¢ as agreed to with the farmer when he bought the future. Then he would have no choice but to sell them at 16¢ and lose 2¢ per pound.

Example No. 3:

This is the reverse of No. 1. Sam goes to Sally first. She says she needs carrots and will pay 25¢ a pound. Sam sells her 500 pounds at that price. He doesn't own them, but he's brash enough to sell them anyway. Now he hunts for a farmer who will sell carrots to him for 20¢ a pound.

The gamble is that maybe he won't find a farmer who has carrots that cheap. Maybe he'll have to buy carrots for 27¢ a pound, then deliver them to Sally at 25¢ and lose 2¢ a pound.

Example No. 4:

This is the reverse of No. 2. Sam goes to Sally and sells her the "future" at 23¢. She likes the idea. No more worries about how high carrot prices might go that summer. She knows hers will only be 23¢.

Come summer, Sam hunts for a farmer who has cheap carrots

—at least cheaper than 23¢ a pound. He finds one who sells carrots for 12¢ a pound. Sam makes a bundle of profit.

The gamble involves the possibility the summer is wet. This causes most carrot crops to rot in the soggy ground. There are only a few decent carrots around. The lowest price Sam can find is 28¢ a pound. He has to buy them and deliver them to Sally at 23¢ a pound. He takes a 5¢ a pound loss. If he doesn't do it, she'll sue him.

Example No. 5:

You and Sam go to the farmer in spring again.

"Want to buy the future once more?" the farmer asks. "My ulcers would like it if I know now what price you'll buy my carrots for this summer."

Sam's not in a gambling mood, but he's tempted. "What if I come back in a few weeks?"

"Okay, but I may have the future sold to somebody else by then. Or my price might go up by then. I hear seed prices could go up. If they do, I'll want a higher price for my carrots."

"I understand," says Sam. "What if we did this, then? How about I give you one cent per pound right now just to keep my chance open for two weeks. If I come back within two weeks, you have to sell me the future for eighteen cents a pound. If I don't come back, you keep the one cent per pound. I pay you now."

The farmer agrees. Sam has paid 1¢ per pound, but not for the carrots. He's only paid for a chance to buy them. That's called an option. Sam now has the option to *buy* the future carrots. And he has the option to *not buy* the future. He has two weeks to use his option.

Here is the gamble: Sam sees Sally. Suppose she says she's already agreed with someone else to buy carrots this summer at 15¢? Sam loses out, but all he loses is 1¢ per pound. By buying an option he made his gamble smaller.

Example No. 6:

You and Sam reverse No. 5. You see Sally in spring. She's anxious to buy a future carrot crop for 25¢ a pound. But Sam's not in a gambling mood. He's not sure he can buy future carrots that cheap.

Finally he says, "I'll give you one cent per pound to keep my chance open for two weeks. If I come back in two weeks, you have to take future carrots at twenty-five cents per pound. If I don't you can keep the one cent per pound."

The gamble: Suppose when Sam sees the farmer he's too late? The farmer already sold his future crop for 29¢ a pound. Sam has to let his option with Sally go by. He loses his 1¢ a pound to her. But it's a small loss because he only had an option.

Many, many things are sold in one of the six ways just described. "Things" that are sold are called commodities. Sugar is a commodity. So is rubber. So is corn. These commodities are bought and sold in markets called exchanges.

Chicago has big exchanges for the grains and animals grown in the Midwest, and you'll find exchanges for different commodities all over the world. Coffee, cocoa, orange juice, wheat, oats, beans, cattle, hogs, potatoes, eggs—all these foods are bought and sold on exchanges. Lumber, plywood, cotton, copper, gold, silver—all these are handled on exchanges, too.

You can pick up a phone today and buy any of these items on an exchange. You can buy or sell the commodity itself—as

Sam did in Examples No. 1 and 2. Or you can buy or sell the "future" crop—as Sam did in Examples No. 3 and 4. Or you can buy an option on "futures"—as Sam did in Examples No. 5 and 6.

Why do we have exchanges and futures?

Imagine you are a baker. You buy wheat for your bread at 2¢ a pound today. Next week the price is up to 8¢ a pound. So you have to double the price of your bread. Two days later the price of wheat drops to 4¢. You still have some 8¢ wheat left, so you can't very well drop your bread price yet. When you don't, your customers get mad. The baker across the street dropped his price, they say. Why didn't you?

Now suppose you can be absolutely sure you can buy wheat 3 months from now for 4¢. You can plan the price of your bread 3 months ahead.

You can buy wheat this way through an exchange. And huge bakeries do just that. They contract to buy wheat in 3 months at 4¢ a pound. The "Sam" they contract with now hunts for a farmer who will sell wheat at 1¢ or 2¢ per pound. If he finds one, he'll make a good profit.

Imagine you're a farmer and grow wheat. When your wheat's ripe this summer you may be able to sell it for 6¢ a pound, or maybe the best price you get will be only 2¢ a pound. But you don't know what the price will be. That's in the future.

If you can sell it at 6¢ a pound, you can get a new tractor. If you earn only 2¢ a pound, you'll have to sell your pickup truck to make ends meet. The trouble is, you don't know *now*. And now is when your neighbor wants to buy your pickup.

Suppose you could know *now* that your wheat will bring 4¢ a pound this summer? Well, you can know this: You can contract now to sell your future crop of wheat for 4¢ a pound.

The "Sam" you contract with will now search for a baker who'll pay 8¢ a pound for it. If he finds one, he'll make a handsome profit.

Millions of tons of commodities are bought and sold on exchanges every day. People like Sam make tremendous fortunes with commodities. And sometimes they lose tremendous fortunes. The people who buy and sell commodities never do it blindly. They learn as much as possible about anything that affects the commodities they handle.

Let's say you buy and sell wheat on the Chicago exchange. You'll find out how many acres are planted this year in a dozen countries. You'll know how much rain falls in wheat areas during this year. You'll know how much bread people are eating this year. You'll know if rail workers are going on strike this summer. (Wheat travels by railroad. Any strike will foul up deliveries.) You'll know a thousand and one things about the wheat crop. The more you *know,* the less you'll be gambling.

8

A LOAN TO MICKEY MOUSE

Remember in Chapter 1, how Mr. Johnson loaned money to a country and that Mrs. Emery loaned money to Disneyland? In order to learn how they did this, let's drop in on the great Me n' Sam Newspaper Company where—to the surprise of no one—Sam is talking again about the need to raise money. This time the need is for $1,000 to buy new machinery.

And this time you're going to raise the money with bonds.

In this manner you borrow money from someone and sign a document that says you promise to pay the money plus interest on a certain date. The document, which has your seal on it to make everything official, is a bond.

Now your company will have ten bonds printed, each promising that the Me n' Sam Newspaper Company will pay $100 to the person who owns the bond ten years from now. And each bond will promise that the company will pay 7% interest to the owner every year. You can attach coupons to the bonds, and these will be good for the interest due each year.

Now you sell the bonds to people. When you sell all ten, you'll have your $1,000. That is, people will have loaned the money to you and your bonds are your promises to repay the loans with interest.

You can pay the interest in various ways. But *how* you pay it doesn't matter here. The important thing to know is that a bond is your promise to pay someone the money he or she is loaning you now.

You tell your friend Mr. Gazekas that you'll soon be offering bonds, and he suggests a mortgage with the bonds.

Remember what a mortgage is? Mr. Gazekas (or his bank) loans $1,000 to you *against* your building. If you don't pay the $1,000, he takes your building. Now Mr. Gazekas and nine others are each loaning $100 to you. You could arrange things so that if you didn't repay the money, your building would become theirs. They could sell it and try to get their money back.

But you're not going to offer a mortgage to back up your promise this time. You're simply going to promise to repay. This means your bonds will be called Debenture Bonds. (Our word "debt" comes from the word "debenture." In Latin "debenture" means "they are due.")

All sorts of companies borrow millions of dollars through bonds. Of course, they have to be healthy companies to do it, for who wants to lend money to a company for ten years if it may not be around after five? Bonds also are the way towns, cities, counties, state—even nations—raise money.

Since governments get money from taxes, why do they have to *borrow* money, too?

Well, your company already gets money from selling its newspapers every day, but it needs $1,000 *now* to buy machinery *now*. It could save up the $1,000, but that would take three years. So it borrows it and will pay it back out of the money it gets selling newspapers every day.

Your state, city, town or village is no different. The state wants $200 million for new roads. The city needs $20 million for sewer repairs. The town wants $2 million to replace old bridges. The village wants $20,000 for new sidewalks.

If they try to save this money out of taxes, they'll be saving for several years. And during those years the roads won't be built, the sewers won't be repaired, the bridges won't be replaced, the new sidewalks won't be laid. So, instead of saving for years, they borrow the money with bonds in order to do the jobs now. Then they pay off the bonds with money they receive from taxes over the next ten years.

Your school system does the same thing—usually for building schools. The system then pays off the bonds with school taxes.

A number of government agencies borrow money this way, too. Your state may, for example, create a department to build apartments for old people and then pass a law making it legal for this department to issue bonds. So the department issues bonds, sells them for money, and then uses the money to build the apartments *now*.

Of course, you have heard of United States Savings Bonds. Millions of Americans buy them. When you buy them, the money you pay goes to the United States government: that is, you are lending money to your government—your country. You lend small amounts by buying U.S. Savings Bonds and you can lend $100,000 or more to your country by buying other types of United States bonds.

You can loan your money to other countries, too. You usually have to have a lot of money to do this, for bonds of this kind are very expensive. Some wealthy people buy bonds from countries all over the world. For example, you may have heard of Israel Bonds. The small country of Israel has borrowed hundreds of millions of dollars through bonds it has sold to individuals in this country.

During World War II, 75 million American citizens bought war bonds. That is, they loaned money to the country so it could wage war. Over half of the money the United States government borrows today, it borrows from individuals.

Incidentally, the government doesn't send you some interest every year on your small bond: It simply sells you a $25 bond for $18.75. If you keep it until it's due, you can cash it for the full $25. The extra $6.25 you made is the interest on the money you loaned the government.

You can join an investment club or group that buys bonds, pooling your money with money from many other members. The club can then buy large bonds that most individuals can't afford, maybe one of those $100,000 bonds.

Banks and savings and loan associations buy bonds. So do companies, universities, foundations, insurance companies. There are several good reasons why both individuals and institutions buy bonds instead of putting their money in a savings bank or buying stocks.

You'll get more interest from a bond than from a bank, so your money will earn more money for you.

You won't have to worry much about the price going up and down. Stock can double in price overnight on the stock market —and it can go down in price just as dramatically.

While bonds are bought and sold like stocks, their prices don't go up and down as much. You can always hang on to them and know exactly what they'll be worth if you keep them until they're due. A stock, of course, doesn't become "due" this way.

You always know how much interest you'll make on a bond. If a bond pays 7% interest, that's what you'll get every year. But stock may pay a 7% dividend one year and only 3% the next. If the company does poorly, there may not be any dividend at all.

Because the United States government guarantees its bonds, a purchaser is not taking much of a gamble when he buys them. Thus the United States government can easily raise 2 billion dollars tomorrow just by announcing it is issuing some new bonds.

If you have a big amount to loan, bonds can be more convenient than stocks. Each stock might be worth $50; if you have $50,000 to invest, you'll have to buy 1,000 different stocks and keep track of them. With bonds, however, you might buy one bond worth $50,000.

Most of the bonds for your country, state, city, or other municipal government are all or partially tax free. This means you won't have to pay taxes on the interest you earn. If, for example, you earn dividends of $1,000 from your stock, you may have to pay $250 of that in income taxes. After all, it is income. But if you earn $1,000 interest from your United States government bonds, you won't have to pay any income taxes on it.

Bonds are bought and sold, like stocks, at an exchange or a

marketplace. You buy and sell them through "brokers" as you would buy and sell stock.

Let's suppose your Me n' Sam Newspaper Company someday borrows $20 million with bonds. And suppose you don't want to mess around with all the paperwork or wait until every last bond is sold, which could take months. You want your money now. You want to spend your time making newspapers, not selling bonds.

To make things easy, you offer to sell the bonds together in a lump sum. When you do, an "investment bank" offers you $19,500,000 for them. You sell them because you're happy to get the money you need now. The bank then sells the bonds in many places over the next 3 months for $20,000,000 and makes a profit of $500,000.

Most company bonds and many government bonds are sold in this way. This is particularly true of state and city bonds, in which amounts of money are so large that the investment bank usually teams up with many other banks when they buy the bonds, thus spreading the risk.

Now you know how Mr. Johnson loaned his money to a country: He bought United States Savings Bonds.

And now you know how Mrs. Emery loaned her money to Disneyland. Disneyland issued bonds so it could borrow money, and Mrs. Emery bought some of them.

9
LEND ME YOUR EAR

You need $200 for a vacation and decide to borrow it. Where is the best place to go for the money?

The best bet is a friend who won't charge interest. But all your friends are hep to interest, so that's no help.

How about a pawnshop? How does a pawnshop work anyway? You go to one and the owner explains. He'll loan you $30 on a $50 radio. "And if you don't pay me back," he says, "I sell your radio for $50 and make $20."

"Do you charge me any interest on the $30 you lend me?"

"No interest."

"So instead of charging interest you're really making a bet that I won't come back?"

"Right."

"If I come back, you lose your bet. If I don't come back, you win?"

"Right! You're a smart kid."

At least you're smart enough to stay away from pawnshops. So on to the finance company—one of those store fronts with a neon sign that proclaims, "Loans! Loans! $100 to $1200." You ask the man at the counter if you can borrow $200.

"Maybe," he answers. "Two hundred dollars, eh? Let's find out something about you first." He asks who you are, where you work, how much money you earn, how much money you have in the bank. He wants to know how many company shares you own and how much they're worth. He wants to know if you are now loaning money to anyone or borrowing any. In short, he wants to know how much you're worth.

Then he asks if you've ever borrowed money from anybody before. You may have had loans from a bank and another finance company. He'll phone them and ask if you repaid the loans as you promised. He may investigate you further.

Finally he's convinced you'll probably pay as you promise. He thinks you're a "good risk." He says, "Yes, we'll be happy to lend you the money. How long do you need to repay it?"

You've been thinking about this. "How about twelve months?"

"Okay."

"How much interest will you charge?"

"Interest? How does eighteen percent sound?"

"Wow! Eighteen per . . . .Wow!"

You have to pay a high rate of interest at a finance company because it loans money to a lot of people who are "poor risks." Banks and savings and loan associations won't lend money to many of these poor risks. So the finance company charges more interest to pay it for taking a big risk. Remember the rule: The greater the risk, the higher the interest.

Often people who borrow from finance companies never repay

the money, and thus the high interest rates they charge make up for these non-payers. Finance companies are not like pawnshops in that you don't have to leave something with them. They do loan money on some things, such as cars. The person who borrows may use the money to buy a car. Then, if he doesn't pay the loan back, the company has the right to take the car and sell it.

"If I borrow money from you, how do I pay it back?" you ask the man at the finance company. "Do I pay the lump sum at the end of the year?"

"We could arrange that. But with most of our loans the person pays us a little bit every month until the loan is paid off."

"Where do you get all this money to lend out?"

"We borrow most of it."

"Do you borrow money from people and companies the way banks do?"

"Not exactly. We simply borrow money and promise to pay it back. We usually borrow big amounts in the big cities, maybe with bonds. Of course, we pay interest on it, just as the bank does. And we lend it out, just as the bank does."

That is, finance companies borrow at low interest and make their profit by lending at high interest.

Remember Mrs. Emery, who, in the first chapter, loaned money to a company one morning for five years, then borrowed money from the same company that afternoon for three years?

Here's how she did it. In the morning she phoned her stockbroker and told him she had $10,000 she wanted to invest. He suggested that she buy debenture bonds from Houseword Finance Company which would fall due in five years and pay

6½% interest. So she loaned her money to Houseword under arrangements made by her broker. That afternoon she decided to buy a car. She went to her nearest Houseword Finance Company office and borrowed $3,000 for three years at 14% interest.

A travel agency sounds like an odd place to borrow money. But that, in effect, is what happens when an airline lends you money to buy its tickets under a "Fly now—Pay later" plan.

They won't hand money to you, but they will let you take many months to pay for your tickets. You'll have to pay interest, too. For example, if you pay cash for the tickets, they cost $200. But if you take 12 months to pay for them, you pay $20 per month, or $240. You've paid $40 extra, or 20% interest.

This is known as retail credit and is a widespread practice. You can, for instance, buy a $300 washing machine from Sears and pay for it over 24 months. In other words, Sears virtually lends you $300 for 24 months. You will pay Sears about 18% interest for the loan. (Sears calls it a finance charge.) Your payments will, of course, add up to much more than $300 because of the interest. If you use the machine but stop payments after 6 months, the company can take the machine away because it owns it until you make all the payments.

Now suppose you bring the washing machine home in January and the first small payment is due on February 10. But you change your mind and don't want to take 24 months to pay it off. On February 10 you take $300 out of the bank and pay Sears the entire amount. You had the machine for a month before you had to pay any money, so Sears has loaned you $300 for one month at no interest because the interest would have started in February. Thus you borrowed $300 for a month and paid no interest for it. Most stores which let you buy "on credit" won't charge interest in the first month.

Where else can you borrow that $200? You can go to a bank, of course, or borrow from a savings and loan association. If you belong to a credit union, you can borrow from it. People there will ask you the same questions the finance company men asked. They want to know if you are a good risk. If you have money on deposit with them (in other words, if you are lending money to them) they are more likely to lend money to you. And they will usually charge less interest than will a finance company or a store.

You've probably seen advertisements for credit cards and seen people use them. How do they work?

Let's imagine that your father owns a store in a shopping center and knows everyone who works there. When you and your mother stop at the various stores in the center, neither of you likes to carry a lot of money and your mother doesn't feel like writing a check for every little purchase.

Your father, wanting to make shopping easier for you, visits all the stores in the center and shows them a fancy card he's had made. It has his name on it, your name, your mother's, and your brother's.

"Anytime a person shows you this card," he tells the people, "you'll know that person is from my family. You don't have to take money from that person. Just write down what he or she buys. Send me the bill. I'll pay you by check."

That is a credit card.

Now, suppose the card doesn't have your father's name on it. Instead it says "Master Charge" or "BankAmericard" or "Visa" or "American Express."

When you show that card at a store, it tells the cashier that she doesn't have to take money from you. She records what you buy and the store sends the bill to "Master Charge" or whomever. Master Charge pays the store by check. Later Master Charge tells you what bills it paid for you, and you pay Master Charge.

Master Charge makes money in two ways:

The store pays Master Charge a small fee on each bill for a couple of reasons. The charge card is so convenient that it encourages people to buy more and thus the store sells more. Also, when a customer buys something with a Master Charge charge card, the store knows that it will be paid promptly by Master Charge. If, instead, the store takes checks from customers, some checks will bounce. There is no chance of that with a charge card, so the store is happy to pay a fee to the charge card people.

Master Charge also charges interest on the money you owe. If you don't pay Master Charge promptly, you pay interest and the money you owe becomes a loan. Master Charge likes to lend money to you in this way and collect a good amount of interest.

Suppose you take your vacation early in January and charge all your $200 in bills on your Master Charge card. Master Charge sends you the bill in early February. If you pay it then, there's no interest. Thus you've borrowed $200 for a month without interest. If everyone did this, Master Charge might go out of business, for it makes most of its profits by lending money at high interest to people who don't pay their monthly charges right away.

People use credit cards for all sorts of purchases—even for hospital bills and veterinarians. They pay funeral directors by credit cards, even taxi drivers. Some people pay their donations to churches by credit card. Many have dozens of credit cards. One man in California collects them for a hobby and had over 900 of them when this book was written. Most of his cards are issued by stores, like Sears and Montgomery Ward. They can only be used for merchandise from those particular stores. Others, from gasoline companies, are only good for gas, tires, oil, and the like at those companies' stations.

You won't need 900 credit cards. Most people get along with just a few or only one. And many get along without any.

10

A WORD ABOUT PROFITS

Many people think that companies make enormous profits on everything they sell. They like to point out, for example, that a food company charges 49¢ for a can of carrots, yet a gardener can grow enough carrots to fill a can for 2¢ worth of seed and a little garden space. Therefore, the food company must be making an outrageous profit on every can of carrots.

In fact, the company probably does buy those carrots for only a few cents. But it has to pay for dozens of things along the way before the carrots get to the grocers' shelves.

Big companies pay for all sorts of things. Most put money away every year for pensions for their employees. They frequently pay for medical insurance for their employees. They pay for research, for experiments on products they may not be able to sell for another ten years.

A carrot producer might spend a lot of dollars to develop a carrot that won't catch diseases, and then it turns out the carrot tastes terrible, so the money has been wasted. Companies usually pay a variety of taxes. They borrow money, and so they pay a lot of interest. They build new factories and design new products. They give money to charity.

After all of these costs, the money left over is the net profit. Companies in America make an average of about 5¢ net profit for every dollar taken in. This is only an average; some companies make 10¢, others make 2¢. Supermarkets make about 24¢ *gross* profit before expenses for every $1 they take in, but after they pay for all the things mentioned above they end up with about 2¢ *net* profit for every $1.

If you're feeling sorry for these companies, you can dry your tears. Let's look at the situation from a different angle.

Consider your and Sam's own newspaper company which *was* making a good profit for this year. But you didn't want to pay a lot of taxes on that profit or pay too much out to the stockholders in one year, so you did a few things to reduce your profit.

The company rents motorbikes for you and Sam, and in December it paid the rent on them for 6 months ahead. That was tricky. Because you made the payment in December it's part of this year's business, though you really borrowed some expenses from next year. You are using these expenses to cut down your profit for this year.

You and Sam also paid yourselves big bonuses, extra money, in December. You made out well, but the company had to dig into its profits to pay the bonuses.

Next, you had the company throw a big Christmas party for all the people who advertise in the papers. That also came out of the profits, naturally.

Then you took yet another step to make your profits look

smaller for the year. You told the paper boys not to collect money for December but to put off collections until January. In other words, you took some of this year's sales and put them into next year's business.

There are other things on which the company spends money that come out of profits. But you and Sam get a lot of personal use out of them and they're not strictly for business.

The company pays for your membership in a tennis club and YMCA or YWCA. It pays for tickets to movies and plays so that you can write about them for the paper. It does the same for football, baseball, and basketball games. It pays for a color television set and a fancy radio. These are for you to hear the latest news for your papers, of course. And the company pays for a beautiful tape recorder for interviewing people who supply news for your papers.

Big companies do the same sort of things in more complicated ways. Some companies even violate laws, though most stay within the law.

Companies resort to such tactics for a simple reason. They don't want to appear to be too wealthy. Many people are uneasy about big profits for companies. They resent them, maybe envy them. If you and Sam dripped with money and bragged openly about profits, many people would no longer be your friends. For this reason it's good for a company to look healthy, but not *too* healthy.

Sometimes, however, a company wants to look *more* healthy than it is.

Suppose it appears your company won't make a profit this year. If it doesn't, it won't pay a dividend; its stock prices will slip when the stockholders find out.

You can pull a few tricks, then, to make the company look more profitable than it is. The company can put off paying for some things. Motorbike rentals will be paid in January rather than December. You can have the paper boys try to collect for January's papers in December and you might offer customers a lower price if they'll pay early. Thus you will steal sales from next year and use them for this year, fattening current profits.

Most of these maneuvers catch up with a company. If they hide profits and losses this year, they will show up next year. There are two important things to remember when you think about profits in big companies:

Don't be fooled by gross profits; net profits are what count. And don't be fooled by tiny profits; companies don't always end up with as tiny a profit as they'd like you to believe.

11

MONEY TO BURN— OR AT LEAST INVEST

Let's suppose you've had a few good years and saved several thousand dollars. You have it in a bank, earning interest, but after a while you feel restless about it and wonder if there aren't other ways of making more money.

You can make a practice of loaning to friends; a lot of people do. You can buy a house and make money from renting it. You may sell it for more than you paid and make money there, too. But don't count on a fortune from being a landlord. Don't forget taxes, insurance bills, upkeep, repairs. Yet don't be easily discouraged, for many people earn a lot of money from owning houses, apartments, office buildings. The point is they have to buy and sell wisely and cope with various expenses.

You can buy and sell property. It's pleasant to think about buying a vacant lot for $2,000 and in six months selling it for $4,000 to a company that needs land for a new supermarket. On the other hand, you can pay $2,000 for a lot no one will buy from you until you finally get rid of it for $1,800.

MONEY TO BURN—OR AT LEAST INVEST

You can invest in many different things besides buildings and land. Some people buy paintings; others buy gold and silver. Some invest in rubies and diamonds and coins, while others buy old books or antiques as investments.

Some people who buy and sell in a matter of weeks or months we call traders rather than investors. An investor will hold some objects for years, sometimes many years. He may buy paintings from an unknown artist for only $50 each and hold them for 20 years until the painter is world famous. The investor sells his $50 paintings for $50,000 each. Or by that time the painter's work may be judged so bad that the investor can only give it away. A wise investor will take great pains to learn all about the books or rubies or paintings he's buying—or hire someone who knows all about them to advise him.

As you know, investment in a bank savings account is better than investment in your shoe. But it's only going to give you a relatively small amount of interest. Most investments will earn more than a savings account. Don't forget, however, that your bank savings are insured and you can earn larger amounts by leaving your money there for longer periods of time.

You can loan your money on a mortgage. Sam buys a $25,000 house, but has only $15,000 of his own. You lend him $10,000 and take a mortgage on the house. Remember, that means if Sam fails to pay, you can claim the house. Sam pays you 9% interest for the $10,000, a nice investment. Sally buys a $25,000 house with $12,000 of her own. She gets a $10,000 mortgage, but still needs $3,000. You lend it to her for a second mortgage. If she fails to pay, you're second in line behind the person or bank that has the first mortgage. Because it's risky,

Sally pays you 15% interest. A profitable investment, but chancy.

You can make a lot of money quickly with commodities. You can lose your shirt, your shoes, even your underwear just as quickly.

You can invest in stocks and bonds in two ways. You can buy and sell quickly, which is really no more than trading. Or you can buy and hold for long periods, earning stock dividends every year. And after many years you may be able to sell the stocks for much more than you will pay today. You could buy stocks of IBM for a few dollars many years ago when the company was young and small, and every $1,000 worth of stock you bought then would be worth hundreds of thousands of dollars today. Stocks are complicated, however. While IBM grew, other companies shrank. You might make a million with stock from IBM but lose two million with stock from W. T. Grant, which went bankrupt. You can both make and lose money with bonds, too. But how do you sort out the good investments from the poor ones? How do you stay away from the W. T. Grants and get close to the IBMs?

You can study the stock market. You can read books and magazines and newspaper articles about it. You can buy newsletters to learn more about it. You can read a million words about various companies like IBM. In other words, you can try to become an expert on the stock market. Or you can hire an expert to advise you or to invest money for you. You can hire a firm of experts whose job it is to study these matters and to invest money for their customers.

You can always join a big group of people for investments.

You can pool your money with theirs. That will give the group a lot of money. The group can then hire some of the best experts to invest the money. (Experts always seem to be expensive.) Some of these groups are called mutual funds. Some are simply investment clubs. In the small groups you can vote for or against certain investments. The large groups have too many members for this.

In the big groups the money is lumped together. Experts are hired. They invest the money and report these investments to the members. Some groups invest only in stocks. Some invest only in particular types of stock, like oil and gas stocks. Some invest only in bonds. Some invest only in particular types of bonds, like tax-free bonds. Some groups invest in land, some in cattle. Each group is different.

Why join a group? One reason is that with experts to do the investing you don't have to learn as much. The experts do the learning and thinking for you. Also, a group won't put all its eggs in one basket. It will invest in dozens or hundreds of stocks or bonds.

Let's say you have $4,000. You invest it in the stock market on your own. That amount won't go far in the stock market today. You can only buy $1,000 worth of stock in four companies. One company, to which we'll give the made-up name Charlie Brown Company, goes broke. You lose the $1,000 you invested in its stock. This is one-fourth of the $4,000 you started with!

Let's say you invest the $4,000 in a mutual fund instead. The fund buys stock of a hundred different companies. Your $4,000 is spread among a hundred companies now instead of four. Charlie Brown Company goes broke. But now its stock is worth only one-hundredth of your $4,000. You're protected.

Uncle Mike received a pension check every month. Not his Social Security check, which was from the government. Uncle Mike got a check every month from the company he used to work for, and he would have got it for the next fifty years if he lived that long. Mike worked for the company 30 years. Each year the company put $1,000 for him into a group investment fund, and the fund hired experts to invest his money in stocks and bonds. When the dividends and interest rolled in, they were invested, too. Over the years the $30,000 invested for Mike grew to $70,000. When Mike retired, he had a choice to make. He could take the $70,000 in one lump, or he could leave it in the fund and take $8,000 per year for the rest of his life. Mike chose the $8,000—and lived 20 more years.

In the past, many retirement funds like these were badly run. When companies went broke their retirement funds went broke, too. People like Uncle Mike lost their pensions. Others lost their pensions because they didn't work quite long enough to qualify. Some got sick a year before they were to retire and because they couldn't work the last year they lost their pensions. Some were fired a year before retirement and lost their pensions, too.

Finally Congress wrote new laws to stop this sort of thing. People are much better protected today. Retirement funds are usually independent from their companies now, and if a company goes broke its retirement fund continues to operate. (For instance, W. T. Grant's pension fund still operates even though the W. T. Grant Company went bankrupt.) Also, if a person works 10 years and leaves a company, he can take his share of the fund with him under new laws. Retirement funds aren't perfect, but they are better now than they were a few years ago.

Institutions such as the Ford Foundation and Rockefeller Foundation give billions of dollars every year to universities, scholars, scientists, and worthy projects. Such foundations were created with large amounts of money and they hired experts to invest the money. The investments earn interest and dividends; some of the stocks a foundation sells are worth twice what it paid for them. Some of these profits are reinvested, while other amounts are used to pay employees and given to worthy causes.

Where does a private college or university get the money to pay its teachers and defray its running expenses? (State colleges and universities get money from state governments, but I'm talking about private schools here like Harvard, Wellesley, Kenyon.)

The money students pay to attend school is not enough for the school to pay its bills. Schools need more money to pay their way. So they ask for donations from foundations, individuals, companies. Usually a school invests cash donations and some of the gifts it receives are in the form of stocks or bonds anyway. The investments earn money, of course, and the school uses the earnings to pay its bills. Some schools have hundreds of millions of dollars invested. Harvard University had $1.4 billion invested as of 1977, and Yale had $568 million. If Harvard received 6% from its investments, it would make $84 million per year.

Here's where the University of Rochester, Rochester, N. Y., had its money invested in 1971.

10.3% — *Bonds*
    Government bonds, Canadian and foreign bonds, utility bonds (gas & electric co.'s etc.), industrial bonds (from companies)

9.6% — *Miscellaneous*
    Included some mortgages

2.9% — *In the bank*

5.0% — *Stocks* of small companies that might grow big

72.2% — *Common stocks* of companies
    These included: 50,000 shares of Walt Disney Studios
      65,000 shares of Avon Cosmetics
      82,000 shares of K mart (S. S. Kresge Co.)
      100,000 shares of MacDonald's (yes, the hamburger chain)
      100,000 shares of J. C. Penney Co.
      100,000 shares of Taylor Wine Co.
      50,000 shares of Caterpillar Co.
      130,000 shares of IBM
      900,000 shares of Xerox Co.
      900,000 shares of Kodak (Both Kodak and Xerox are Rochester companies and Taylor Wine Co. is located nearby.)

Many wealthy people pay all their living expenses with money their investments earn. For example, a couple may have $200,000 invested at about 8% in interest, dividends, and the like, which gives them $16,000 per year to live on. Not-so-wealthy people do it, too. Someone like Uncle Mike will take his retirement fund in a lump sum of $70,000, invest it at 8%, and have an income of $5,600 (8% $\times$ $70,000) per year. That added to his Social Security check, enables him to live fairly comfortably.

If you live in a Communist country, you might not be allowed to have investments like these. In some countries only the government owns companies, so there are no shares to buy and sell.

In some countries only the government owns houses; you cannot lend money as a mortgage on a house then. You probably can put money in a government bank that pays some interest, but most of the other things we've discussed are forbidden in Communist countries.

Not all Communist economies are the same. For instance, in Poland you may have your own business, but you are allowed to have only a few employees. And some "collective" or community businesses and farms return profits in one form or another to the workers—who are similar to stockholders. Private enterprise is not absolutely forbidden under Communism, but it certainly is frowned upon.

We live under a "private enterprise" system, which means "private investment." It means that you and Sam, as private individuals, may own a company such as you do and invest your own money in an enterprise to earn more money.

Investing is more widespread in private enterprise countries now than it was 50 years ago. Then, only the wealthy owned stocks and bonds and mortgages; now more people have them. This is because so-called common people have more spare money now than they had then. They're paid more for their work and it's easier for them to invest. There are mutual funds, investment clubs, retirement funds, investment experts to whom they can go with their money.

The non-Communist world would grind to a halt in a week if investments were made illegal. For our schools, our cities, our government, our companies operate on money that people invest in them.

You'll recall that Amy Brown in Chapter One saved $2,000 per year for 30 years. That should have added up to $60,000 when the 30 years were up, but it added up to a whopping $245,000. This was because Amy invested her money wisely over the years. She bought some good bonds, invested in some excellent stock, bought some mutual funds, gambled with commodities once in a while, loaned some of her savings to friends at good interest rates.

Whenever she received any interest, she immediately invested that new money somewhere. When she made a profit on a commodity, she invested that, too. When she received a stock dividend she did the same. Over the 30 years her investments averaged 8% profit, or 8% interest per year. Believe it or not, after 30 years this gave Amy $245,000 for retirement!

12

INFLATION

Your little company hums along nicely with your employees producing hundreds of papers every week and (before there was a change in the Minimum Wage Law) receiving wages of $3 per hour. You sell the papers for 25¢, and the wages you pay the printers and writers amount to 10¢ per paper. This leaves you 15¢ per paper with which to pay your other expenses.

But then one day the printers and writers go on strike for more money. You and Sam negotiate with them and eventually agree to pay them an extra 60¢ per hour. This increases your labor cost per paper by 2¢. Until now there was 10¢ worth of labor in each 25¢ paper, but now there is 12¢.

Next day the delivery boys, hearing that the printers and writers got a raise, go on strike. So you negotiate with the delivery boys until they agree to accept 3¢ more for each paper they deliver. Adding this to the 2¢ more you now pay the printers and writers means that the cost of your papers has jumped by 5¢.

Hold the phone. The newsprint company feels it needs more profits and raises its paper prices. You have to pay 1½¢ more for the newsprint in each copy of your paper. So the cost of your paper is now up by 6½¢.

Are you receiving anything more for the 6½¢? Are the printers and writers making more papers during their work hours? Now that you pay more for a roll of newsprint, do you get more papers from it? Do the delivery boys deliver more papers than before? The answer is, of course, no. You must do something about this problem right away. So you raise the papers' price by 7¢. The papers were 25¢, but now they'll cost 32¢.

Sally buys four of these papers every week: one for her mother, one for herself, and two for her fruit and vegetable store. When the price of your papers was 25¢, Sally's dollar bought four of them. That is, her dollar was *worth* four papers. But now her dollar buys only three papers—it is *worth* only three papers. So, when it comes to buying papers, her money is *worth* far less than it was a week ago.

Suppose this happens to many of the dollars Sally spends. First, the price of her papers goes up 7¢. The papers grew no larger, are delivered no more quickly, carry no more news than before. But they cost 7¢ more.

Next, food prices rise for her. Bread rises 5¢, milk 5¢, hamburger 15¢. Her money grows weaker, it lessens in buying power. Two years ago $20 bought 5 days' worth of groceries for Sally, but today $20 buys only 3½ days' worth.

Sally's money suffers from inflation. When prices "inflate," they enlarge. But her money does not.

What causes inflation? Not everyone agrees on an answer. One thing on which most experts agree, however, is that higher salary without more production contributes to inflation. You experienced this with your newspapers; you had to pay people more money than before to produce the paper, but they did not work faster or harder in return. They did not *produce* more for the extra money you paid. This will contribute to inflation, as Sally can tell you from personal experience.

Sally sees prices rise for her papers, her food, her clothing. Deciding she needs more spending money to cope with these rising prices, she raises the prices at her fruit stand.

Local teachers feel these higher prices, too, and their union asks the school board for 10% pay raises. Other people in other jobs begin to do the same thing. Now inflation is under way in earnest.

I don't mean to single out unions as the only culprits in inflation. Company managers can start inflation snowballing by arbitrarily raising prices merely so that their firms will make fatter profits. Arab oil companies did this a few years ago. They believed their stocks of oil would run out in 20 years and felt they needed more money for their oil now, to invest in other industries in the meantime. When companies grow inefficient they, too, fuel inflation. They spend unnecessary money making their products. To recover this wasteful spending, they must raise the prices of their products.

Legitimate shortages also add to inflation. If half of America's wheat crop is wiped out by drought this year, the price of wheat will skyrocket. The prices of all foods made from wheat will also climb.

To understand how inflation pinches, suppose I give you $100 every week to spend any way you wish. You accept the deal and decide to spend $50 per week to buy a house, $25 for food, $10 for your motorbike and $5 for clothing. That leaves you with $10 per week for saving. You think you're sitting pretty—and you are, for a while.

Six months pass. Gasoline goes up in price, and because of this you now have to pay $12 per week to run your motorbike. Clothing prices rise, and now clothes cost $7 per week. These increases leave only $6 per week you can save. Still, you're comfortable. You pay your various living expenses and have money left over.

Another six months pass. Food prices rise by another $5. The interest rate on your house mortgage goes up, and now you must pay $55 per week instead of $50. You need $105 per week to cover your expenses, but you only receive $100.

What do you do? First, you probably use some of your savings. Second, you start spending less. Perhaps you eat less, buy less clothing, walk more and motorbike less.

Another year passes. Prices all rise again. What do you do now? Perhaps you sell your motorbike. Perhaps you sell your home.

Now you know what inflation does to old people. Most of them receive pensions that never grow, like your $100 per week. They also receive Social Security payments from the government. These, at least, grow larger to try to help them cope with inflation, but Social Security payments don't always go up as much as prices do.

How much has inflation weakened the dollar in this country? The $100 that would buy four weeks' worth of groceries 35 years ago will buy one week's worth today.

Remember Mr. Johnson in the first chapter? When he retired, he counted the $2,000 in twenty-dollar bills he saved in the very first year he started saving. It was still $2,000, of course, just as it was 30 years before. At the same time it wasn't anywhere near as much as it was 30 years ago.

Now you know why. Inflation marched on while his $2,000 snuggled for 30 years under his mattress. Had Mr. Johnson invested his $2,000, it might have kept pace with inflation and have grown to $6,000. This $6,000 would buy today what his $2,000 would buy 30 years ago. Alas, he didn't invest his $2,000, and so today he has the same $2,000 with which he started. But it won't buy even half what it would 30 years ago.

You can see now why you are wise to invest your savings. If you don't—and inflation takes place—your money grows weaker. Each time inflation steps forward, your money stands still.

In 1977 the inflation rate in the United Kingdom was 16% per year. In some Latin American countries it was 30%, even 50% per year. That meant if your salary was $10,000 in 1977, it would have to be $15,000 in 1978 to keep pace with 50% inflation.

13
BANKRUPTCY

Suppose your company is going bankrupt. Why? For too long it spent more than it earned. Instead of making more money, you borrowed more money. You and Sam ignored the telltale signs.

Bankruptcy occurs when you cannot pay your bills. Either you go to a court and tell this to a judge or the people to whom you owe go to court and tell the judge they don't think you can pay your bills.

There are two good reasons for declaring bankruptcy: To get your creditors—the people to whom you owe money—to stop pestering you. And to gain the right to start over again. For, if the judge allows you to become bankrupt, you can be freed from your debts.

Your creditors will go to court because they know you have some property left. Suppose, for instance, you have mimeograph machines, paper, offices, desks, motorbikes and the like. If the judge says you're bankrupt, he'll have all these things sold, then divide the money from the sale among the various creditors.

Let's say your company owes $10,000 and the sale of all the company's property raises $5,000. The court divides $5,000 among the creditors. This means they will only receive $1 for every $2 you owed them. It's not much, but it's better than nothing.

Meanwhile the judge frees your company from its bills. Your company is finished, but you and Sam aren't bankrupt personally. You were merely employees of the company; you lose your jobs and the money you spent on the shares of stock.

Bankruptcy is the way a company tosses in the towel. It is the way creditors make a company call it quits. It is also the way a person can quit and start again. For a person can declare bankruptcy, too.

He does this by letting his own bills grow much larger than his assets. (Assets are the things of value one owns.) He lets his bills grow so large that he can't pay them from the money he earns.

Thousands of companies go bankrupt every year in this country, and thousands of people do, too.

There is plain old "we're broke" style bankruptcy, as described above, when the court has all your assets sold and divides the money that comes in among your creditors.

And then there is reorganization "give us a breather" bankruptcy. In this you say something like this to the court:

"Our company is only sick. It's not going to die. It can recover and make money again. *But* in order to help it recover, we have to try some surgery. We'll put two of our newspapers up for sale. We'll cut down on the number of people who work for us. We'll sell our motorbikes. We'll fire some of our deadheads and we'll hire some whiz kids. We'll move to other offices that cost less to rent. In order to do this we need time. And we can't have these creditors breathing down our necks. They're hounding us for money. If you could just keep them away from us for a while, we'll get the company back on its feet. Then the company will make money again. And then we'll pay off those old bills."

This is called reorganization. A court can allow you to do this under the bankruptcy laws. But there's one tiny catch. Your creditors have to agree to it. Don't forget, your company owes them a lot of money, and if they agree to let you "reorganize," your company might grow even more sick.

Right now they can get $1 for every $2 you owe them, if your assets are sold immediately. If the company grows more sickly, they may get only 10¢ for every $2.

Your creditors say no; they tell the court they want your assets sold now. You "go bankrupt." Everything is sold to pay your company's bills.

Now what happens? When everything was sold, it only raised enough money to pay half of your debts; your creditors received only $1 for every $2 you owed them. Do you still have to pay the other $1 to them?

No, you don't. First of all, you and Sam don't pay because it was the company that owed the money. You and Sam didn't owe any money. Now the company is no more; it is gone.

Second, even if you started the company again, it wouldn't have to pay the old bills. The company went through bankruptcy, and its debts are now canceled.

The same thing happens when people—individuals—go bankrupt. Various things they own are sold. The money goes toward their bills, and after that all bills left over are canceled.

Many great companies started in the ashes of bankruptcy; many people rise from bankruptcy to stunning success. Of course, some never learn a lesson from their bankruptcy, but fail again and again.

Incidentally, you *may* even be able to borrow again from people who were holding the bag when you went bankrupt. You *may* be able to buy supplies from that paper company that lost $500 when you went bankrupt. If your new company looks healthy, your old suppliers may want to deal with it.

Remember in the first chapter Mr. Johnson and his bankrupt grocery store? Next day Mr. Johnson surprised his friends. He bought a new car and new clothes and traveled to Europe.

Now you know how he did it. The store was in the form of a company, and the *company* went bankrupt. The *company's* assets were sold to pay something toward the bills, but Mr. Johnson's personal property was protected. After all, he was not the company, he only worked for it. He happened to own it, just as you and Sam owned part of your company. When the company was sold, he lost the money he had invested in it. But the creditors couldn't touch his savings account—the court couldn't have his car or house sold. Mr. Johnson happened to have saved a lot of money over the years, and that's what he spent to go to Europe in style.

You and Sam had the same experience. Everything your company owned was sold, but that's where the bankruptcy stopped. You were stockholders, so you lost your stock in the company. The stock is worth nothing now because the company is worth nothing.

This would not be true if you and Sam did not have a company. If you had published the newspapers as partners only and been forced into bankruptcy, you both would have to go bankrupt personally. Then you would lose your bicycle, your savings—everything in order to pay your bills.

It's for this reason there is a type of businessman who "owns" very little. He arranges to have his house and cars and bonds all owned by his wife. When his businesses go bankrupt, he is personally liable. When the court counts up what he owns, however, it finds he owns almost nothing—his wife owns it all. The court can't make her sell anything; she doesn't have to pay her husband's bills.

Many years ago there were no bankruptcy laws, and a debtor was saddled with his bills until he paid them. There was no relief. Today he can wipe the slate clean and start again.

14
WHAT NOW?

You know something about your economic system now; you know more about money than you did. I suggest that you read more. There are many good books on money, stocks and bonds, commodities.

Keep your ears open. You will hear people talk about school bond issues and dividends and foreclosures on mortgages—and you will know of what they speak.

Keep thinking about the things you have read here. Sometime in your life you are likely to have a sizable lump of money. You might inherit it; you might receive it for an insurance claim. You might win a prize. Maybe someday you'll get a big bonus at your job or for signing up in the armed forces. You might receive a generous gift from someone. Or you could save a lot from your salary.

So many people spend that lump of money when it comes

their way. They would be smarter to invest it, but they are afraid of investments—often out of ignorance. If you feel the urge to spend when your lump arrives, I suggest you invest the money and spend only the income it produces. This way you will preserve the original lump, the capital. And it will continue to produce income for you, perhaps for the rest of your life and your children's lives.

At some time you may come across a security or an investment you don't understand. Try not to be awed by it just because it sounds complicated. No matter what it is, it is almost certain to be a tool by which someone or some organization borrows money from others. It is almost certain that the borrower will pay, in one way or another, for the privilege.

This is the basis for the millions of financial transactions going on in the world at the moment.

Remember, money alone will probably not make you happy. But you can gain much satisfaction by making good and profitable use of whatever money you happen to possess.

INDEX

Annual report, 53, 54, 65

Bankruptcy, 106-10
Banks, 19-31, 40
   special types, 21-23, 28-29
Board of directors, 54
Bonds, 75-79
   debenture, 76, 83-84
   interest on, 75-76, 78, 79
   investing in, 94-95
   prices of, 79
   tax free, 79

Chairman of the board, 54
Checking accounts, 34-35

Checks, 33-36
   bounced, 34
   certified, 35
Commodities futures, 68-72, 73-74, 94
   options on, 71-72
Commodity exchanges, 72-73
Communist economies, 99
Companies, 51-67
   and bankruptcy, 108-10
   forming, 51-52, 67
Company directors, 54
Credit card, 85-87
Credit unions, 29

Deposits, 20-21, 27-28
Depression, 27-28
Dividends, 52, 53-54, 55, 63, 65-66, 79
Dow Jones Average, 61
Down payment, 41-42

Endorsement, 33

Federal Housing Administration (FHA), 42
Finance charge, 84
Finance company, 82-84

Inflation, 101-5
Interest, 20-21, 23-27, 29-30, 35
   on bonds, 75-76, 78, 79
     compound, 30-31

INDEX

   on loans, 82, 84
   rates, 23-25
      long-term, 25-26
      on mortgages, 42-47
Investment banks, 80
Investment clubs, 95
Investors, 93
Israel Bonds, 78

Lending, 16-18
Loans, 20-21, 24-25, 75

Master Charge, 86-87
Money, 13-15
   borrowing, 21, 23, 29, 40, 81-87
   investing, 92-100, 105, 111-12
   lending, 16-18, 23, 37-38, 80
   saving, 16, 19-21, 27-28, 30, 35, 93
Mortgages, 38-47, 76, 93-94
   second and third, 46-49
Mutual funds, 95-96

Pawnshops, 81-82
Pension funds, 96
Private enterprise system, 99-100
Profits, 30
   bank, 20, 21
   company, 52, 55, 88-99
   net, 89, 91
Property, 92

Reorganization, 108
Retail credit, 84-85
Retirement funds, 30-31, 96

Savings and loan associations, 28, 40
Savings banks, 28-29
Shares *see* Stocks
Stock averages, 61
Stock exchanges, 58-60
Stockholders, 52-54
    annual meetings, 54
Stocks, 51, 52-67, 79, 94
    buying, 59-60, 83-84, 94
    common, 65, 66
    investing in, 94-96
    issuing new, 62-63
    prices of, 55-58, 60-62, 64-65, 79, 90-91
    preferred, 65-66
    splitting, 66-67

Takeovers, 63-65
Traveler's checks, 36

United States Savings Bonds, 77-78, 79

Veterans Administration (VA), 42

War bonds, 78

Youth Banks, 22

The Author

Tom Morgan is a businessman and writer who has written technical manuals for the Bendix Corporation, helped publish a Navy newspaper in Antarctica, and written for newspapers, radio, and television. After service in the Navy he moved to New Zealand where he married a schoolteacher and worked in advertising. In 1970 he and his wife brought their three children to the United States. Now they live on a small farm in upstate New York where they grow big gardens, which they try to get their children into and keep their sheep out of.

LIBRARY
THOMAS A. EDISON SCHOOL

332.024 M	DATE DUE			7.95
Johnson				
DEC 2 '83				

332.024   **Morgan, Tom**
M   Money, money, money
                      X57605